Happy Kanako's Killer Life

2

story & art by:
TOSHIYA WAKABAYASHI

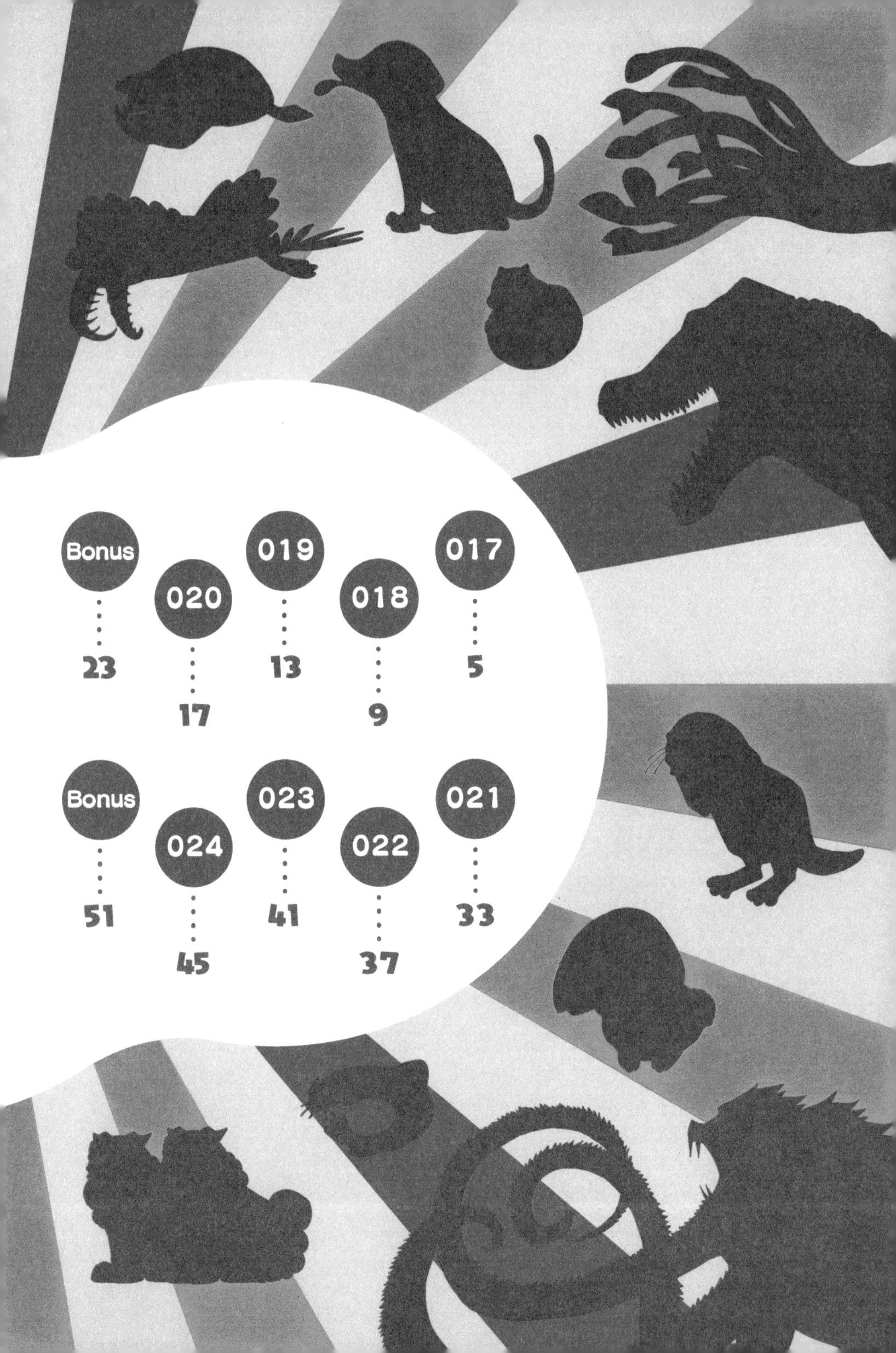

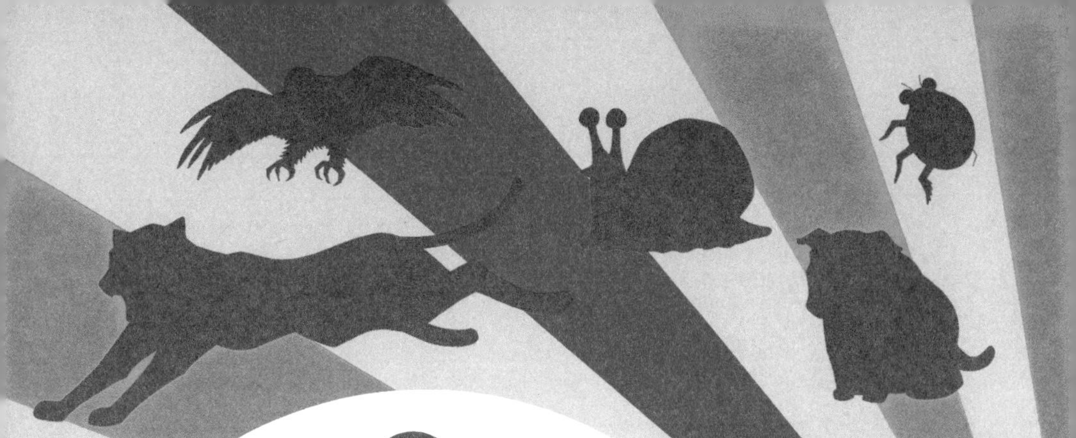

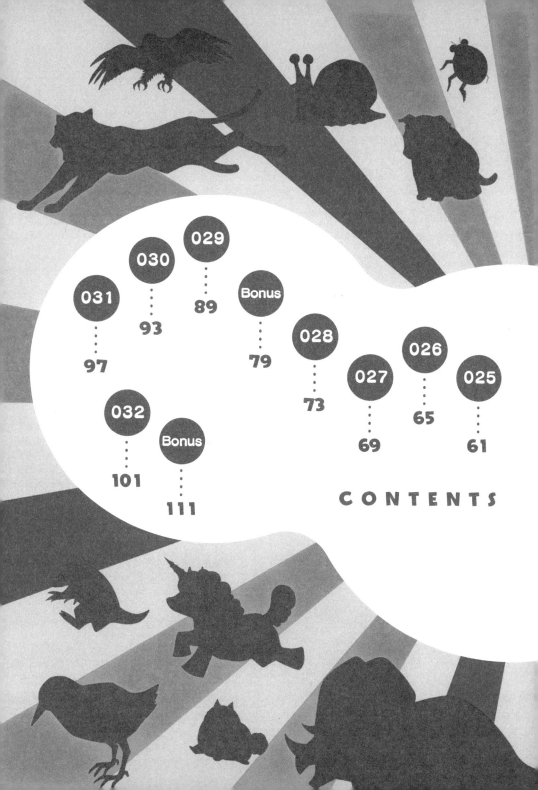

CONTENTS

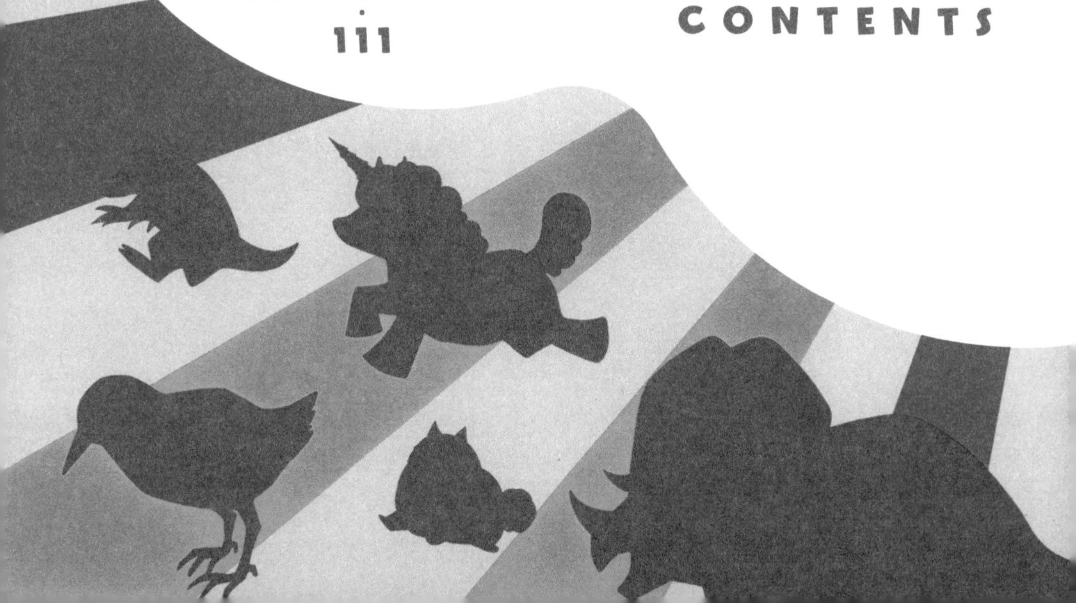

Happy Kanako's
Killer Life

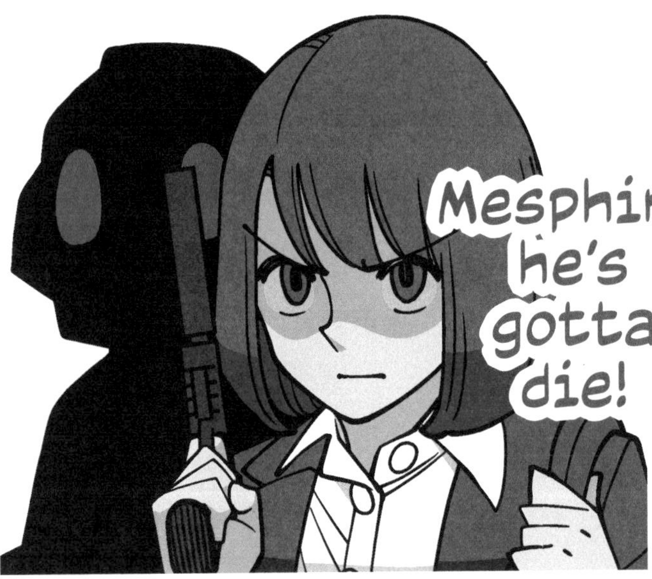
Mesphinx he's gotta die!

017

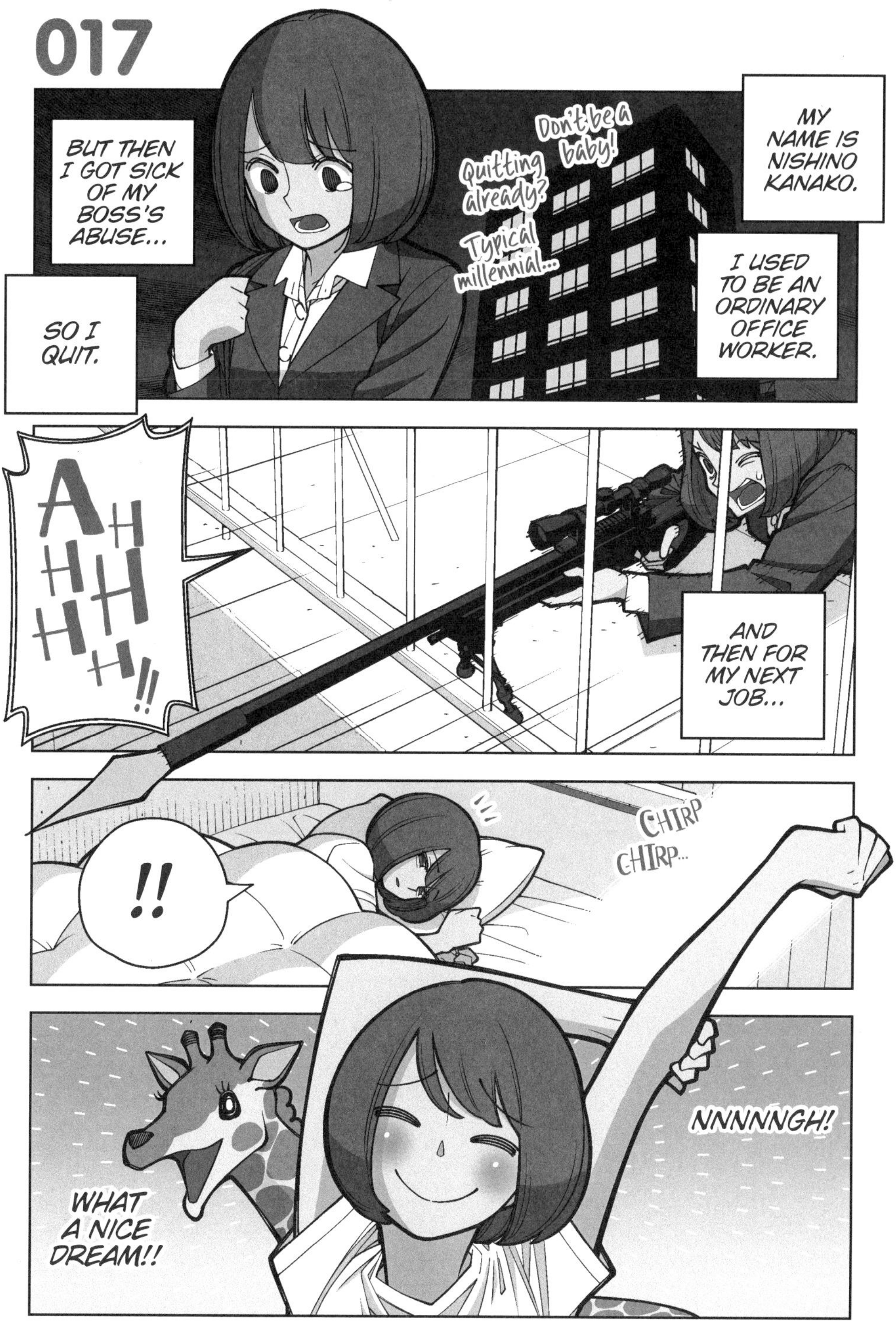
MY NAME IS NISHINO KANAKO.
I USED TO BE AN ORDINARY OFFICE WORKER.
Don't be a baby!
Quitting already?
Typical millennial...
BUT THEN I GOT SICK OF MY BOSS'S ABUSE...
SO I QUIT.
AND THEN FOR MY NEXT JOB...
AHHHHHHH!!
CHIRP CHIRP...
!!
NNNNNGH!
WHAT A NICE DREAM!!

It's the circle of life. ☆

AH!!

MY WORK MADE THE NEWS!!

I'M TWO MONTHS INTO BEING A HITMAN.

I FEEL LIKE I'M GETTING THE HANG OF THINGS.

Yi News

YouTuber Murder Vi: Gone Viral

...vasion of wild tanuki

I NEVER IMAGINED GETTING PUBLIC RECOGNITION LIKE THIS.

THAT MY LIFE WOULD JUST BE BORING.

I ALWAYS THOUGHT...

I DEFINITELY CAN'T TELL MY MOM OR MY FRIENDS.

BUT...

BUT IT'S STILL AMAZING!!

I GOTTA SCREENSHOT THIS!!

☆ ——————————————— **She's really hamming it up!**

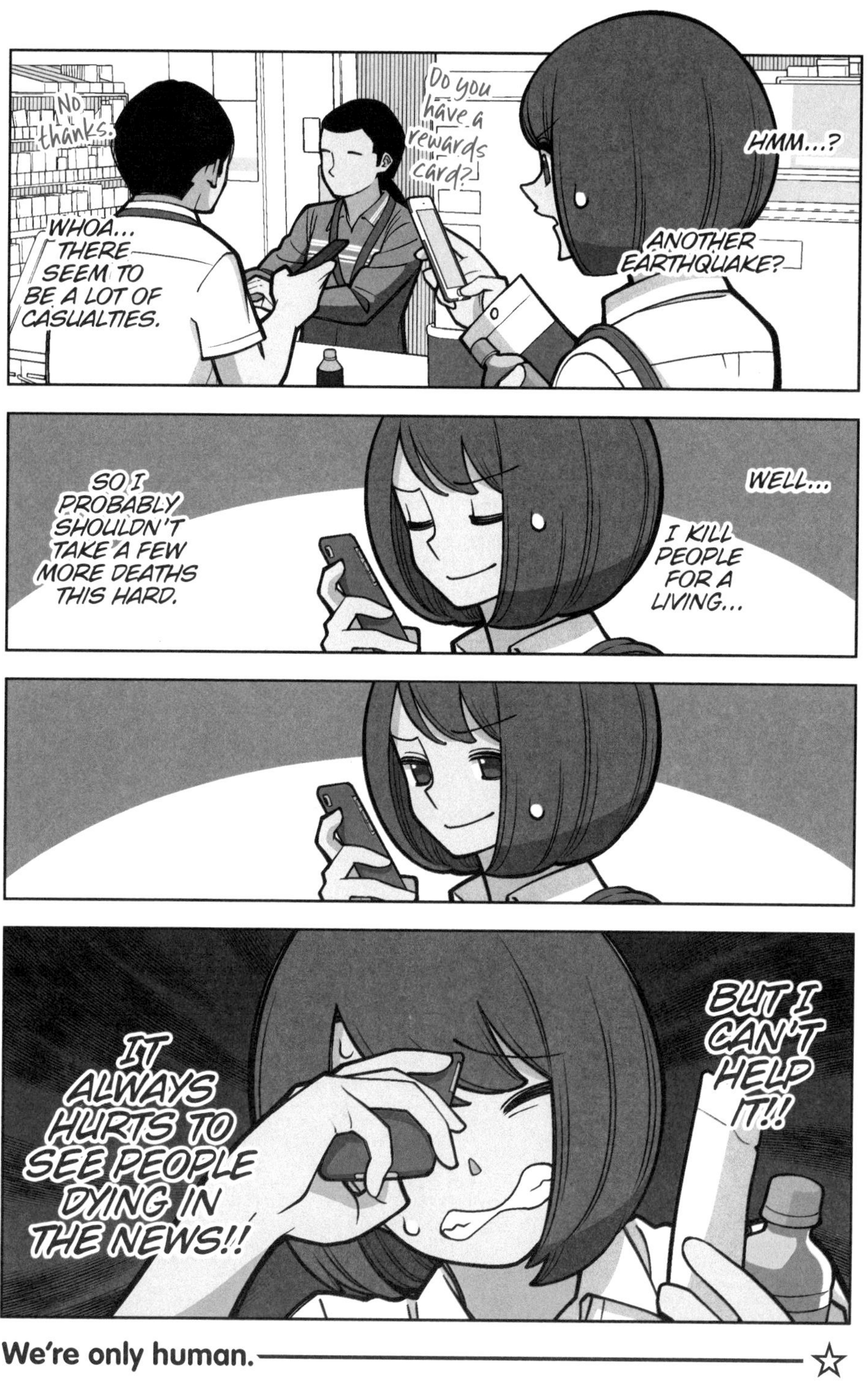
HMM...?
ANOTHER EARTHQUAKE?
Do you have a rewards card?
No thanks.
WHOA... THERE SEEM TO BE A LOT OF CASUALTIES.
WELL...
I KILL PEOPLE FOR A LIVING...
SO I PROBABLY SHOULDN'T TAKE A FEW MORE DEATHS THIS HARD.
BUT I CAN'T HELP IT!!
IT ALWAYS HURTS TO SEE PEOPLE DYING IN THE NEWS!!

We're only human. ☆

THIS WORLD IS JUST FILLED WITH SADNESS.

IS THERE ANYTHING I CAN DO ABOUT IT...?

I WONDER...

JUST SOME OLD DUDE I TOOK A PIC OF!!

SERIOUSLY?! WHO'S THAT THUG IN THE PICTURE?

DID YOU HEAR ABOUT THE EARTHQUAKE?

I STARTED A RUMOR ABOUT LOOTING IN THE AREA!!

I wonder how many people fall for it this time, lulz.

ANY WAY I CAN!!

I'LL JUST HAVE TO DO MY BEST.

Sending a pic of the target. Method is up to you.

How many hoaxes does that make?

SIGH...

NO POINT GETTING FRUSTRATED.

I'M GIVING IT MY ALL!

P.SHEW P.SHEW

OKAY!!

ANOTHER DAY, ANOTHER CHALLENGE.

☆ ──────────────── **Swing for the fences!**

It'll be the bulldog blues if that happens. ⎯⎯⎯⎯⎯⎯ ☆

THE BOSS IS OUT.

HE WON'T BE COMING BACK IN TODAY.

BUT SAKURAI-SAN DOESN'T SEEM TO LIKE ME THAT MUCH.

OH... THE BOSS KINDA SORTA APPRECIATES ME...

WHAT IS IT?

SOMETHING YOU WANT TO TALK ABOUT?

MAYBE YOU WANT TO TELL ME?

I'M FINE! IT'S NOTHING!!

OH NO NO NO NO!!

☆ —————That'd lead to a whole warren of problems.

Taking full responsibility until final delivery. ────── ☆

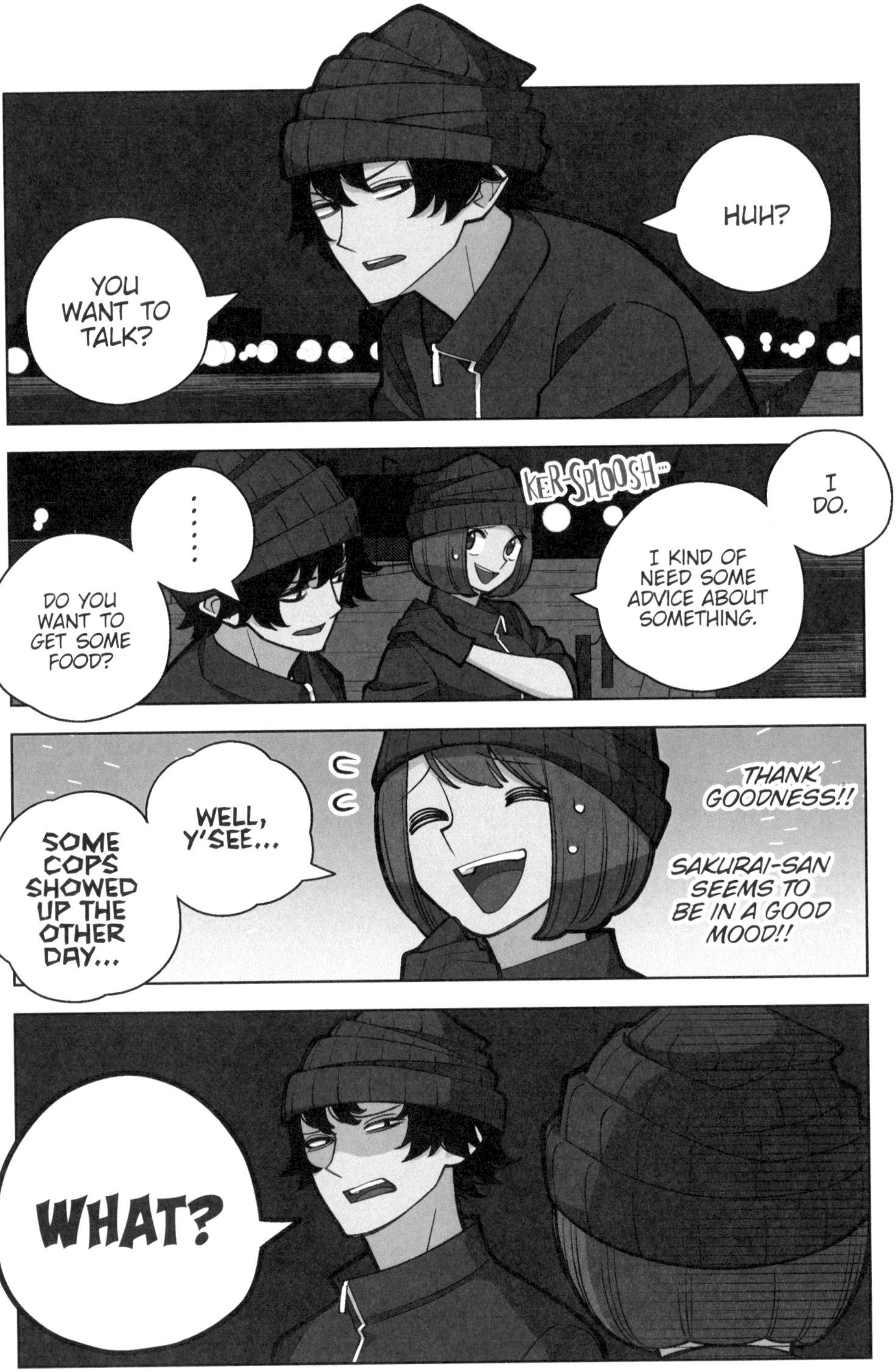

HUH?
YOU WANT TO TALK?
I DO.
I KIND OF NEED SOME ADVICE ABOUT SOMETHING.
KER-SPLOOSH...
......
DO YOU WANT TO GET SOME FOOD?
THANK GOODNESS!!
SAKURAI-SAN SEEMS TO BE IN A GOOD MOOD!!
WELL, Y'SEE...
SOME COPS SHOWED UP THE OTHER DAY...
WHAT?

☆ —— I know, right?

I TOLD MY BOSS.

HE KNOWS ALL ABOUT THE THING WITH THE POLICE.

SO THEY KNOW IT WAS MURDER, HUH...?

MAYBE THEY WERE JUST CHECKING UP ON PEOPLE.

SEEING WHO MIGHT HAVE HAD A GRUDGE AGAINST YOUR OLD BOSS.

BUT IF THEY THOUGHT **YOU** DID IT...

THEY WOULD HAVE BEEN MORE CAGEY.

FIRST THING IS TO PLAY IT COOL.

GO ALONG WITH THE INTERVIEW.

THEN...

WHAT SHOULD I...?

I KNEW THE BOSS WOULD UNDER-STAND!!

HOORAY!!

He's such a pal-amute! ─────────── ☆

WE APPRECIATE YOU COMING OUT TO MEET US.

FIRST OF ALL, I'D LIKE TO THANK YOU.

WE JUST WANTED TO ASK A COUPLE QUESTIONS.

THIS MAY ALL FEEL A LITTLE WEIRD, BUT NO NEED TO FEAR.

JUST CALM DOWN...

OKAY, HE TOLD ME HOW TO GET THROUGH THIS!

Now then, let's see...

THEY DON'T KNOW I'M THE KILLER.

LOOKS LIKE BOSS WAS RIGHT...

DO YOU HAVE ANY HOBBIES OR INTERESTS?

SO...

☆ ———————————————— **Is this a marriage interview?**

I THOUGHT I MIGHT LIGHTEN THE MOOD...!!

OH, UH! EHEH! YOU JUST SEEMED A LITTLE TENSE.

KIND OF EMBARRASSING FOR SOMEONE MY AGE, I KNOW!!

UM... I'M INTO SUPERHERO SHOWS AND STUFF...!!

TH-THAT SURE SURPRISED ME...

I THOUGHT HE MIGHT BE FISHING FOR SOMETHING.

ESPECIALLY THE GUNS!

OH YEAH!!

I USED TO HAVE THOSE TOYS WHEN I WAS A KID!!

?!

Gun ———————————————— Shy. ☆

SORRY... HUH? OH!!

A-HEM!

SHALL WE GET BACK ON SUBJECT?

DO THEY ACTUALLY KNOW... THAT I FIRED THE SHOT...??

You said you quit because of abuse from your former boss.

WHY DID HE BRING UP GUNS...?

PRAWN-HAPS I SCREWED UP??

YES, MA'AM...

TAKEHARA-KUN.

BUT I STILL HAD SOME QUES-TIONS...

SHE'S WHITE AS SNOW.

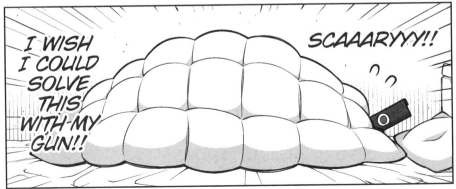

I WISH I COULD SOLVE THIS WITH MY GUN!!

SCAAARYYY!!

☆ ─────── **Face: bone white. Soul: pitch black.**

020

MY MOTHER HAS BEEN WORRYING.

How are things going? Are you eating enough?

Are you enjoying the new job?

AFTER TELLING HER I SECRETLY SWITCHED JOBS...

MAYBE I SHOULD THINK ABOUT CHANGING JOBS AGAIN.

I DON'T WANT TO WORRY HER ANY FURTHER.

OBVIOUSLY I CAN'T TELL HER ABOUT THE WHOLE KILLING-PEOPLE THING.

OR ABOUT THE WHOLE POLICE-INTERVIEW THING.

BECOMING A HOUSEWIFE.

SO REALISTICALLY, THAT LEAVES...

BUT I DON'T THINK I COULD GO BACK TO A REGULAR OFFICE JOB.

NO ONE WOULD TAKE ME!!

HA!! LIKE THAT'D HAPPEN!!

De-Nile isn't just a river. ─────────── ☆

☆————— If only the real world had a block button.

Drugs are no laughing matter. ────────────────── ☆

THAT THIS JOB IS SO EASY.

Welcome back.

IT'S BECAUSE I'M A TIMID, PLAIN, BORING WOMAN...

HOLD UP, MARMOSETTLE DOWN.

C'MON! NO NEED TO BE SO DILIGENT!

I'M STILL ON THE CLOCK.

ACTUALLY...

HMM? ARE YOU NOT GOING TO DRINK?

AH HA, HA, HA, HA...!!

HA HA HA HA HA!!

AH HA HA HA HA HA HA

☆ ──────────── This job rewards diligence.

Happy Kanako's
Killer Life

Fancy
beetling
you
here!!

Happy Kanako's
Killer Life

I'm feeling all squirrely !!

Bonus

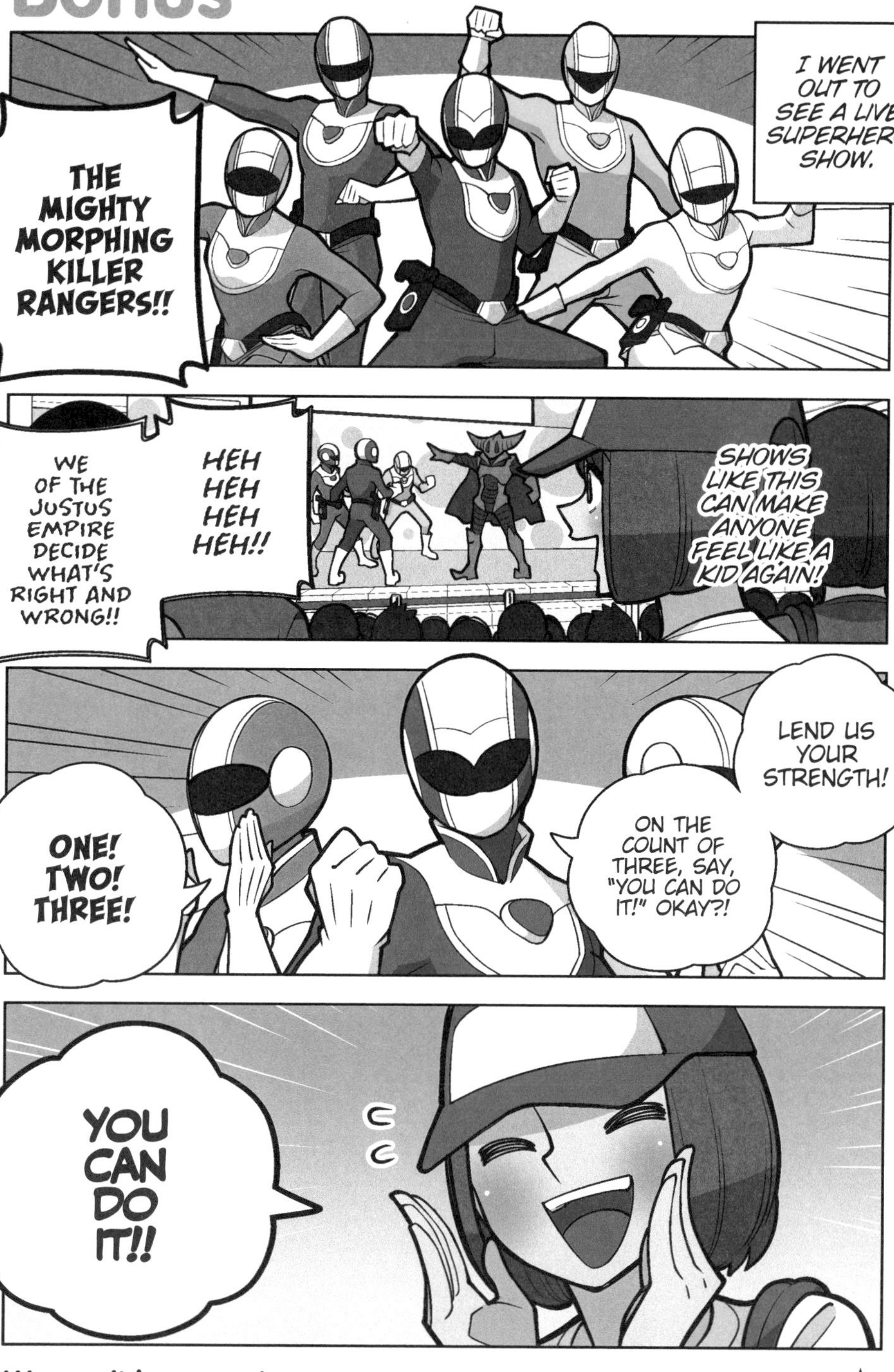

I WENT OUT TO SEE A LIVE SUPERHERO SHOW.
THE MIGHTY MORPHING KILLER RANGERS!!
SHOWS LIKE THIS CAN MAKE ANYONE FEEL LIKE A KID AGAIN!
HEH HEH HEH HEH!!
WE OF THE JUSTUS EMPIRE DECIDE WHAT'S RIGHT AND WRONG!!
LEND US YOUR STRENGTH!
ON THE COUNT OF THREE, SAY, "YOU CAN DO IT!" OKAY?!
ONE! TWO! THREE!
YOU CAN DO IT!!

We can't hear you! ☆

THE SHOW ENDS, AND IT'S BACK TO REALITY.

EVERYONE ELSE IS HERE WITH THEIR KIDS.

LOOKING AROUND...

OH WELL.

IT'S NOT LIKE THERE'S SOME RULE AGAINST GROWN-UPS COMING SOLO.

THOUGH I GUESS IT IS KINDA AWKWARD.

HOW WONDERFUL FOR THEM.

GETTING MARRIED, HAVING KIDS...

I JUST CAN'T SEE THAT HAPPENING FOR ME...

NISHINO-SAN!!

 — **Please save me, Killer Rangers.**

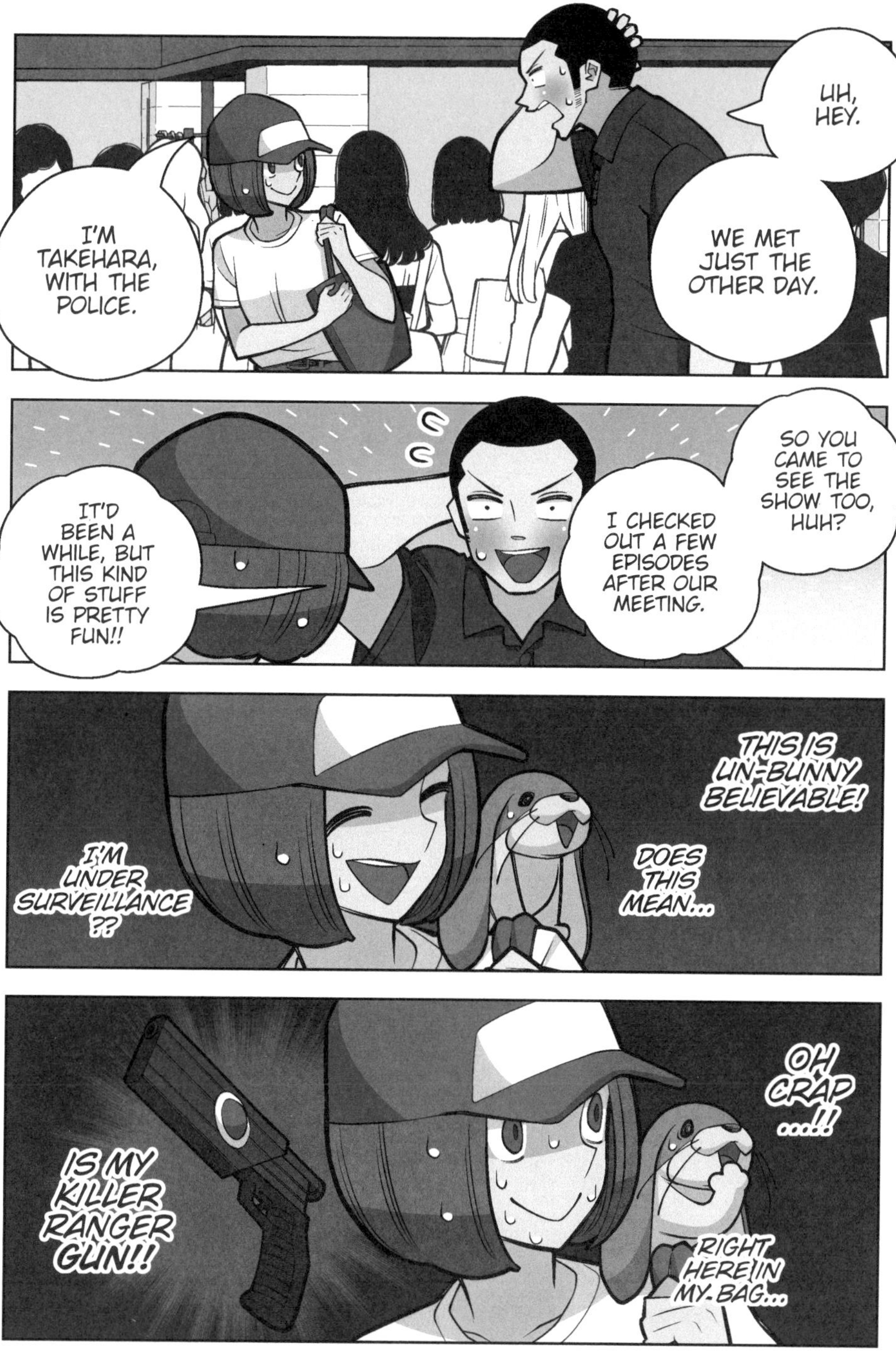
UH, HEY.
WE MET JUST THE OTHER DAY.
I'M TAKEHARA, WITH THE POLICE.
SO YOU CAME TO SEE THE SHOW TOO, HUH?
I CHECKED OUT A FEW EPISODES AFTER OUR MEETING.
IT'D BEEN A WHILE, BUT THIS KIND OF STUFF IS PRETTY FUN!!
THIS IS UN-BUNNY BELIEVABLE!
DOES THIS MEAN...
I'M UNDER SURVEILLANCE ??
OH CRAP ...!!
RIGHT HERE IN MY BAG...
IS MY KILLER RANGER GUN!!

That's an awfully dangerous toy.——☆

ARE YOU GOING TO GET SOME LUNCH?

MAYBE I COULD JOIN YOU...?

HUH? UH...

BUT IF I TURN HIM DOWN, THAT MIGHT BE SUSPICIOUS.

NO CHANCE IN SHELL!!

HE'S DEFINITELY DIGGING FOR SOMETHING!!

I GUESS I CAN BE A BIT SCARY...

UH... SORRY...

NAH... NOT AT ALL...!

IS HE ASKING IF I THINK THE POLICE ARE SCARY?!

☆ ————————————————— **Not scared one bit.**

He's either got sharp instincts or is completely clueless. —— ☆

BEING A DETECTIVE MUST BE ROUGH!!

OUT WORKING EVEN ON A SUNDAY!

ANYWAYS.

OH NO!!

I'VE GOT TO CHANGE THE SUBJECT!!

THEN WHY'D YOU WANT TO TALK WITH ME...?

REALLY?

UH... NO...

I'M NOT HERE FOR WORK.

I JUST...

WELL, THAT'S...

JUST A REALLY AWFUL LIAR?

HUH...?

IS THIS GUY...

☆ ——————————— Pot, meet kettle.

THANKS TO MY WORK...

I'M ALWAYS SEEING THE DARKER SIDE OF THE WORLD.

AND SOMETIMES I GET SICK OF IT.

THAT FEELS PRETTY LUCKY, Y'KNOW?

WHEN YOU FIND SOMETHING YOU CAN GET LOST IN...

BUT SOMETIMES...

AND EVEN THOUGH YOU HAD IT PRETTY ROUGH...

YOU SEEM TO BE HAPPY NOW.

BECAUSE YOU'VE FOUND SOMETHING THAT EXCITES YOU.

Exactly. ─────────────────────── ☆

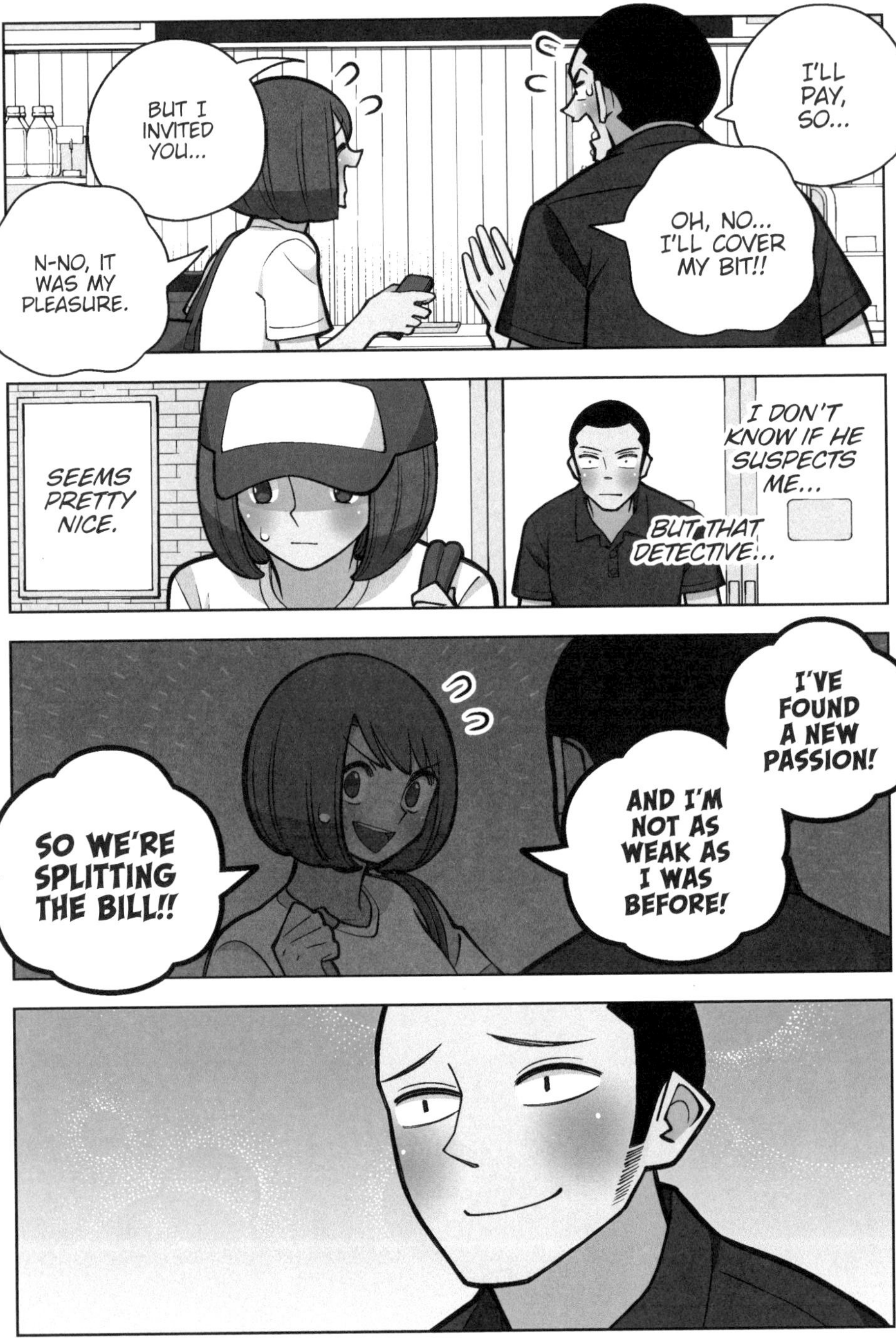
I'LL PAY, SO...
OH, NO... I'LL COVER MY BIT!!
BUT I INVITED YOU...
N-NO, IT WAS MY PLEASURE.
I DON'T KNOW IF HE SUSPECTS ME...
BUT THAT DETECTIVE...
SEEMS PRETTY NICE.
I'VE FOUND A NEW PASSION!
AND I'M NOT AS WEAK AS I WAS BEFORE!
SO WE'RE SPLITTING THE BILL!!

☆ —— Hooked on a feeling.

Happy Kanako's
Killer Life

I'd be
lion
to say
I'm not
jealous.

Happy Kanako's
Killer Life

Cat's out of the bag!!

Are you in love...

with... Takano?

LIFE HAS SETTLED DOWN A BIT.

BUT ALL THIS TIME ALONE IS A BIT DE-PRESSING.

BUT, MAYBE IT'S NOT OUT OF THE QUESTION.

LIKE THERE'S ANYONE OUT THERE WHO LIKES ME, THOUGH...

RELATIONSHIPS, HUH?

I NEVER THOUGHT I'D WORRY ABOUT THAT.

Maybe, given the chance...

we could meet up again sometime!!

THAT WAS JUST HIM BEING PROFESSIONAL.

NO WAY.

"Maybe Next Time" is just business speak for never ever. — ☆

HUH?

YOU MET UP WITH THAT OFFICE LADY??

TAKEHARA-KUN...

YOU KNOW WHAT THAT SOUNDS LIKE, RIGHT?

I DIDN'T "MEET UP" WITH HER!!

WE JUST HAPPENED TO RUN INTO EACH OTHER!!

I'M TRYING NOT TO THINK ABOUT HER WHILE AT WORK...

BUT SHE KEEPS COMING UP.

BUT MY INSTINCTS.

THEY'RE TELLING ME SHE'S IMPORTANT.

I'VE GOT TO STAY FOCUSED.

☆ ——————— **So close, and yet so far.**

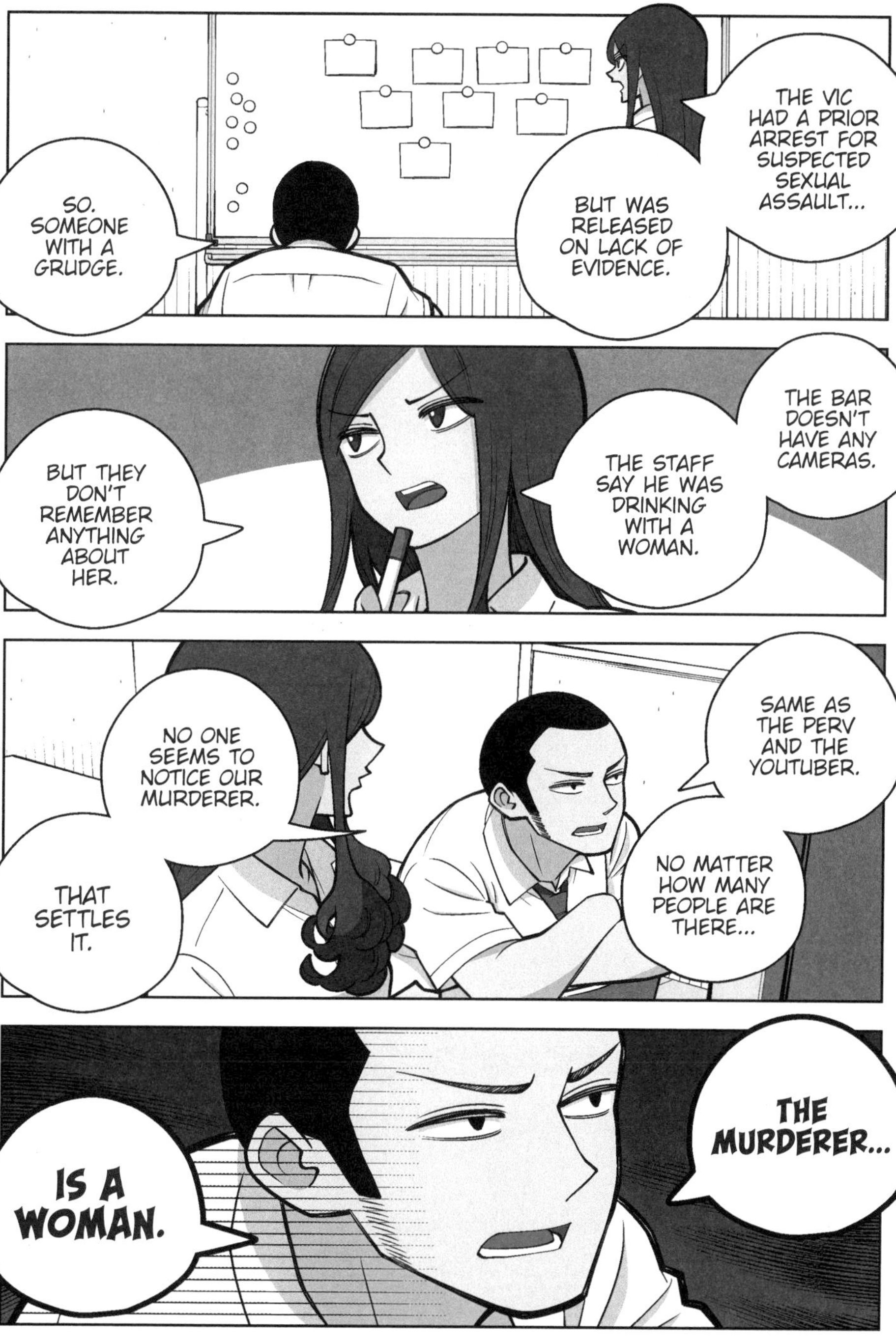
THE VIC HAD A PRIOR ARREST FOR SUSPECTED SEXUAL ASSAULT...
BUT WAS RELEASED ON LACK OF EVIDENCE.
SO. SOMEONE WITH A GRUDGE.
THE BAR DOESN'T HAVE ANY CAMERAS.
THE STAFF SAY HE WAS DRINKING WITH A WOMAN.
BUT THEY DON'T REMEMBER ANYTHING ABOUT HER.
SAME AS THE PERV AND THE YOUTUBER.
NO MATTER HOW MANY PEOPLE ARE THERE...
NO ONE SEEMS TO NOTICE OUR MURDERER.
THAT SETTLES IT.
THE MURDERER...
IS A WOMAN.

Ding ding ding ding! ☆

HUH?

YOU MEAN NISHINO-SAN?

SO?

WHAT'S SO SPECIAL ABOUT THIS GIRL?

AFTER WE TALKED A BIT, SHE'S A LOT MORE SPIRITED THAN SHE SEEMS.

I MEAN, THAT WAS MY FIRST IMPRESSION TOO, BUT...

SHE SEEMED REALLY TIMID.

IS THAT YOUR TYPE?

MEN JUST THINK YOU'RE BORING.

I GUESS IF YOU SHOW YOUR TRUE SELF UP FRONT...

NOT WHILE DOING THIS JOB!

MUNCH

CRUNCH

LIKE I'D EVER FIND ANYONE!

☆ **Eating ice cream in bed is something you can only do while single.**

022

LATELY, MY MOM'S BEEN BUGGING ME...

WHAT?

NO, IT'S NOT THAT I DON'T WANT TO...

ABOUT GETTING **MARRIED.**

No possible candidates there?

Didn't you say the new job was nice?

I'LL KILL YOU.

NOT REALLY.

NAAAH.

An office full of bad guys! ──────────── ☆

MARRIAGE?

WHAT ARE YOU ON ABOUT NOW?

DID YOU HAVE SOMEONE IN MIND?

WELL, THERE'S NO **RULE** AGAINST IT.

BUT IT WOULD BE DIFFICULT.

NO, THERE ISN'T ANYONE.

I WAS JUST WONDERING HOW IT WOULD MESH WITH WORK.

NO WAY, THAT'D BE THE WORST!!

WHAT?!

WOULD BE SOMEONE IN THE SAME LINE OF WORK, RIGHT?

I'D SAY THE BEST OPTION...

RIGHT?

SAKURAI-SAN?!

☆ ───────────────────────── **Right.**

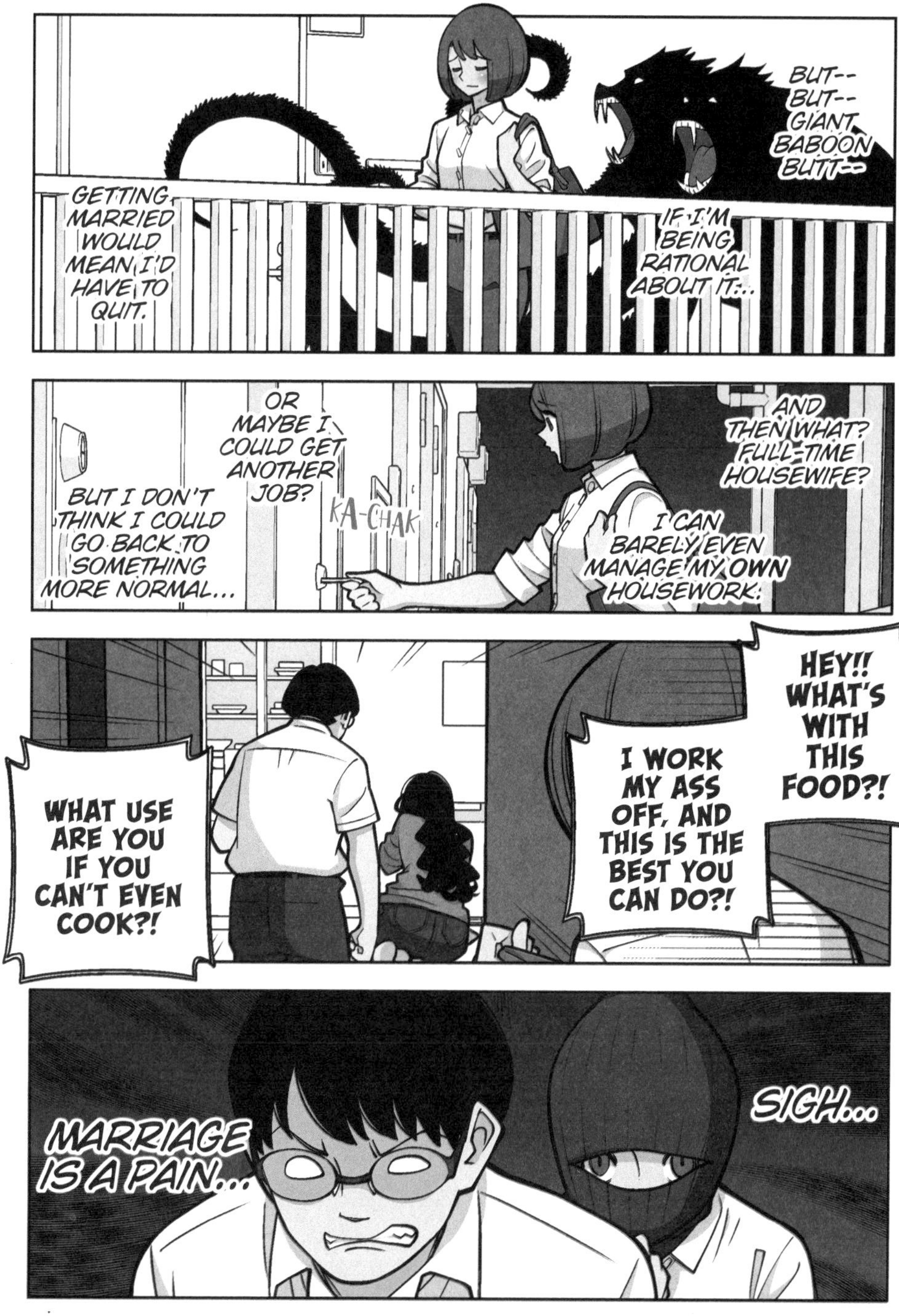
BUT-- BUT-- GIANT BABOON BUTT--
IF I'M BEING RATIONAL ABOUT IT...
GETTING MARRIED WOULD MEAN I'D HAVE TO QUIT.
AND THEN WHAT? FULL-TIME HOUSEWIFE?
I CAN BARELY EVEN MANAGE MY OWN HOUSEWORK.
KA-CHAK
OR MAYBE I COULD GET ANOTHER JOB?
BUT I DON'T THINK I COULD GO BACK TO SOMETHING MORE NORMAL...
HEY!! WHAT'S WITH THIS FOOD?!
I WORK MY ASS OFF, AND THIS IS THE BEST YOU CAN DO?!
WHAT USE ARE YOU IF YOU CAN'T EVEN COOK?!
SIGH...
MARRIAGE IS A PAIN...

Getting married just to be a domestic slave sure would suck! ☆

NOW LISTEN.

THIS IS SET UP TO LOOK LIKE AN ACCIDENT CAUSED BY OVERDRINKING.

YOU SHOULD CALL AN AMBULANCE ABOUT AN HOUR FROM NOW, AND--

HUH?

ARE YOU ALL RIGHT??

I'M FINE... I'M SORRY... IT'S JUST...

I WAS REMEMBERING OUR YEARS TOGETHER...

WEIRD... DESPITE ALL THE ABUSE AND TORMENT...

I GUESS SHE STILL LOVED HIM...?

THIS WHOLE MARRIAGE THING...

IT ISN'T EASY, IS IT?

☆ ———— She never sheds a tear after killing someone.

023

I WENT OUT AGAIN WITH MY ONE AND ONLY FRIEND:

YOSHIOKA KIYOMI-CHAN!

MARRIAGE?

I HAVEN'T REALLY THOUGHT ABOUT IT.

WHATEVER HAPPENS, HAPPENS.

I'M NOT THAT WORRIED ABOUT IT.

YOU'RE NOT ANXIOUS?

LIKE YOU'LL MISS YOUR CHANCE OR SOMETHING...?

SO MARRIAGE ISN'T EVEN REALLY ON MY MIND.

AND I LIKE MY CURRENT JOB...

NOW *THAT* I UNDERSTAND!!

Right on the nose! ─────────────── ☆

NOT TO MENTION THERE'S NO GUY IN THE PICTURE.

THAT'S TRUE.

I'M WITH YOU. IT'S NOT THAT I DON'T **WANT** TO GET MARRIED, BUT...

I'M STILL THINKING ABOUT MY CAREER...

BUT IT'S NICE TO KNOW SOMEONE FEELS LIKE ME.

THERE'S STILL THE PRESSURE OF NOT GETTING MARRIED...

THAT'S A RELIEF...

BETTER FIND A GUY QUICK, RIGHT?!

ALMOST PAST YOUR SELL-BY DATE, AREN'T YOU??

YOU'RE **THIRTY-FOUR**??

DOOOOOOM

 Under Pressure.

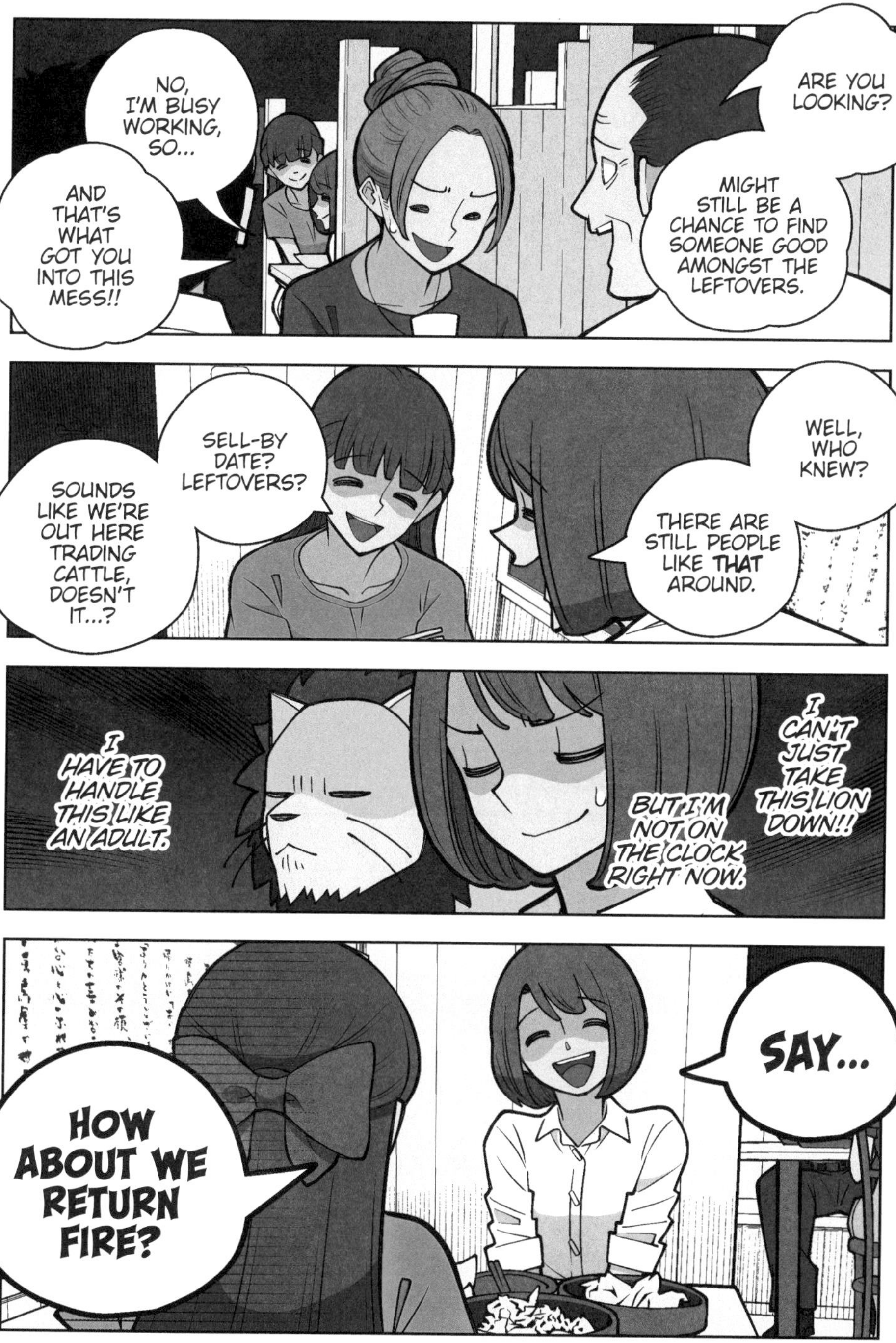
ARE YOU LOOKING?
MIGHT STILL BE A CHANCE TO FIND SOMEONE GOOD AMONGST THE LEFTOVERS.
NO, I'M BUSY WORKING, SO...
AND THAT'S WHAT GOT YOU INTO THIS MESS!!
WELL, WHO KNEW?
THERE ARE STILL PEOPLE LIKE **THAT** AROUND.
SELL-BY DATE? LEFTOVERS?
SOUNDS LIKE WE'RE OUT HERE TRADING CATTLE, DOESN'T IT...?
I CAN'T JUST TAKE THIS LION DOWN!!
BUT I'M NOT ON THE CLOCK RIGHT NOW.
I HAVE TO HANDLE THIS LIKE AN ADULT.
SAY...
HOW ABOUT WE RETURN FIRE?

Occupational Hazard. ☆

Packing a sniper rifle in her heart.

024

NO POINT FRETTING OVER MARRIAGE.

I'LL JUST ENJOY THE SINGLE LIFE FOR A WHILE.

PHEW, I'M BUSHED!

MAYBE WATCH A MOVIE...

CLICK

JUMP IN THE BATH...

ENJOY A DRINK WITH SOME SNACKS...

Eeeek! ⎯⎯⎯⎯⎯⎯⎯⎯⎯⎯⎯⎯⎯⎯⎯⎯ ☆

☆ ———————————— **Show yourself, you little black terror!**

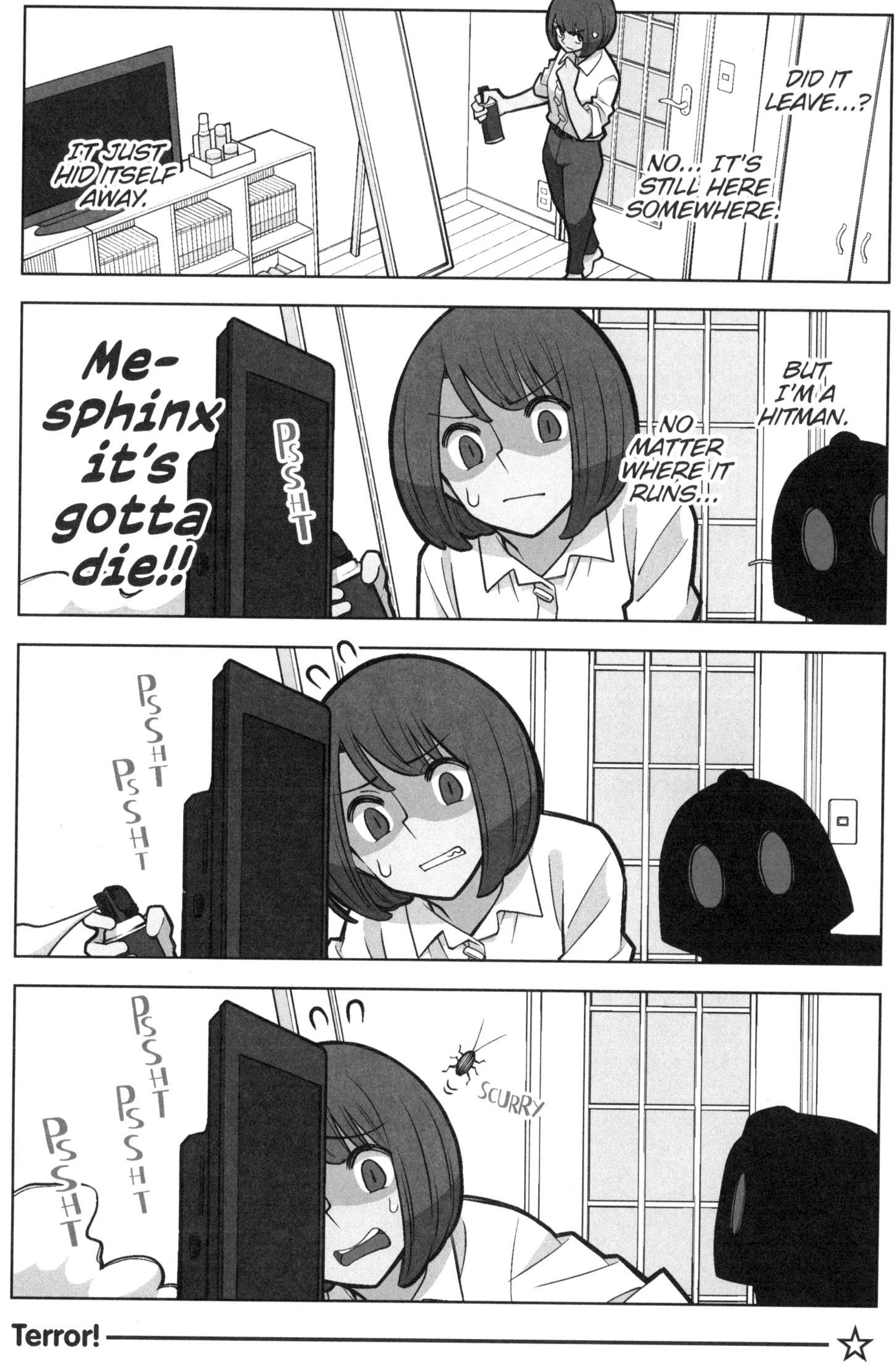
DID IT LEAVE...?
NO... IT'S STILL HERE SOMEWHERE.
IT JUST HID ITSELF AWAY.
BUT I'M A HITMAN.
NO MATTER WHERE IT RUNS...
Me-sphinx it's gotta die!!
PSSHT
PSSHT
PSSHT
PSSHT
PSSHT
PSSHT
SCURRY

Terror! ☆

IT WASN'T THERE.

I SPRAYED EVERY NOOK AND CRANNY...

AND I COULDN'T DRIVE IT OUT.

IT CAN'T BE...

IS IT ONE STEP AHEAD OF ME...?!

WHEREVER IT IS, IT'S PERFECTLY HIDDEN!!

HOW CAN I LOSE TO A SIMPLE ROACH?!

DANG IT!!

OH WELL...

THIS'LL DO IT.

FWOOOOOO

 Thank you, local pharmacy.

Happy Kanako's
Killer Life

Happy Kanako's
Killer Life

Let's
marmo-
settle
down.

Bonus

HMM?

WHAT'S UP?

SO I CAME TO WORK TO HOLD OUT TILL MORNING.

AND THERE AREN'T ANY TWENTY-FOUR-HOUR PLACES IN MY NEIGH-BORHOOD.

WELL, UH... THERE WAS A COCKROACH IN MY APARTMENT.

I KNOW, RIGHT...?

EHEH HEH...

KER-CHAK

AN ASSASSIN, AFRAID OF A LITTLE BUG?

CRAP...

I WANNA GO HOME...

Senpai's just as scary! ⟶ ☆

 — **Is this really the place for that?**

N...NO NO NO...

I HAVEN'T PUT THAT MUCH THOUGHT INTO IT AT ALL!!

IT'S HARD TO DO A JOB LIKE THIS WITH A FAMILY.

SO IF YOU'RE THINKING YOU WANT TO GET MARRIED AND HAVE KIDS...

BESIDES, GETTING MARRIED WHILE BEING A HITMAN...

THAT'D BE WAY TOO CAREFREE!!

WOW!!

I WASN'T EXPECTING THIS LECTURE FROM HIM!!

WHAT ARE YOU TALKING ABOUT?

DON'T YOU KNOW THE BOSS IS MARRIED?

Yep, he's married. ──────────────────────── ☆

★ ———————— Too many landmines in this conversation.

AND THE LAST GUY WHO TRIED TO FIND OUT...

I HAD TO CLEAN UP THE MESS.

I HAVE NO IDEA WHO SHE IS.

HE KEEPS THAT SECRET.

SO IF YOU WANT TO GET MARRIED, GO AHEAD.

THIS IS A LONELY PROFESSION.

SOMETIMES THAT DRIVES PEOPLE TO WANT A FAMILY.

IT MAKES IT EASIER FOR US TO CONSIDER MARRIAGE, RIGHT?

THEN WITH THE BOSS AS AN EXAMPLE...

I SEE...

NOT FOR ME.

That seems clear. ⎯⎯⎯⎯⎯⎯⎯⎯⎯⎯⎯⎯⎯⎯⎯⎯⎯ ☆

THE BOSS HAS BEEN TRAINING ME SINCE I WAS A KID.

I'M USED TO THE ISOLATION.

R... REALLY...?

HAVE YOU BEEN FEELING LONELY?

IS THAT WHY YOU'RE THINKING ABOUT MARRIAGE?

WHAT?! NO...

I JUST THOUGHT IT SEEMED NICE...

JUST DOING THE JOB...

JUST GETTING MARRIED...

IS THAT WHAT MAKES YOU HAPPY?

☆ ─────── **Am I happy living the hitman life?**

It sure was stressful at the start, though! ─────── ☆

AH...

SORRY ABOUT THAT...

CLUNK...

DON'T WORRY ABOUT IT.

WATCHING AFTER YOU IS PART OF THE JOB.

ARE BOTH FINDING THEIR OWN HAPPINESS.

←See you.

I SEE...

SO, THE BOSS AND SENPAI...

THAT MAKES *ME* HAPPY...?

BUT WHAT IS IT...

WELL, WHATEVER!

FOR NOW, IT'LL BE PLAYING AROUND IN THE EMPTY OFFICE!!

☆ ——————————————— **I'm prancing on air!**

Happy Kanako's
Killer Life

Deep breath, count to tenrec!!

Happy Kanako's
Killer Life

025

Best part of growing up is buying all the stuff you wanted as a kid. ☆

IT'S HARD TO COME UP WITH STUFF.

BUT WHEN I THINK ABOUT WHAT I'D LIKE TO BUY OR DO...

I'VE GOT MONEY...

BUT, WHAT WOULD MAKE THIS JOB EASIER...?

English Conversation
19,800 yen

I GUESS IF SOMEBODY FORCED ME TO CHOOSE, I'D WANT SOMETHING TO HELP WITH WORK.

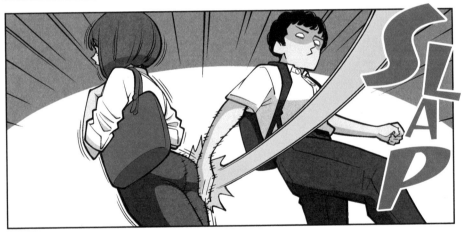

SLAP

SWAGGER

SWAGGER

☆ ——————————— Whoa, whoa, what the hawk?!

Not as spry in your late twenties as you are in your teens! – ☆

Call the station staff!!

↑ Wait... is he dead?!

↑ Huh... what?!

HUFF... HUFF...

AND I'M THIS EXHAUSTED.

JUST A BIT OF POWER WALKING...

JUST LOOK HOW FLABBY MY UPPER ARMS ARE.

IT'S BEEN A WHILE SINCE I'VE PUSHED MYSELF LIKE THAT.

SPEAKING OF, I HAVEN'T BEEN EXERCISING MUCH LATELY.

Find your ideal body shape!
Open 24 Hours Year-Round

Beginner Sign-Up Campaign

▶ 5,980 yen

Sports Gym

I CAN'T KEEP GOING ON LIKE THIS...

I'VE BEEN GOING OUT FOR YAKINIKU AND RICE ALL THE TIME, SNACKING AND BOOZING AND EATING CAKE.

MAYBE...

I'LL JOIN A GYM!!

☆ ———— She's more focused on shape than fitness.

026

TO MAKE USING THE GYM WORTHWHILE...

I ALSO HAVE TO CHANGE WHAT I EAT.

THESE PROTEIN DRINKS ARE REALLY GOOD!

WHAT ARE YOU ON ABOUT...?

NO, WELL...

I WAS JUST THINKING I'D START DOING SOME EXERCISING, Y'KNOW?

ARE YOU ON A DIET?

GIVE IT YOUR BEST.

YOU'VE DEFINITELY BEEN PUTTING ON SOME EXCESS MEAT LATELY.

AAAAGH!!

GAAAH!!

Fat Burning In-Fur-No! ━━━━━━━━━━━━━━━ ☆

HUFF... HUFF...

I SUCKED AT EXERCISING BACK IN SCHOOL...

BUT IT'S ONLY GOTTEN WORSE AS AN ADULT...!!!

AT LEAST COMPARED TO BACK THEN, I'M SWEATING MORE, AND THAT FEELS GOOD!!

QUICK BREAK, AND THEN ON TO ANOTHER MACHINE.

HEY THERE, MISS!!

ARE YOU A NEWBIE??

ANYTHING YOU NEED HELP WITH?

GETTING RID OF YOU.

YEAH...

Swipe left.

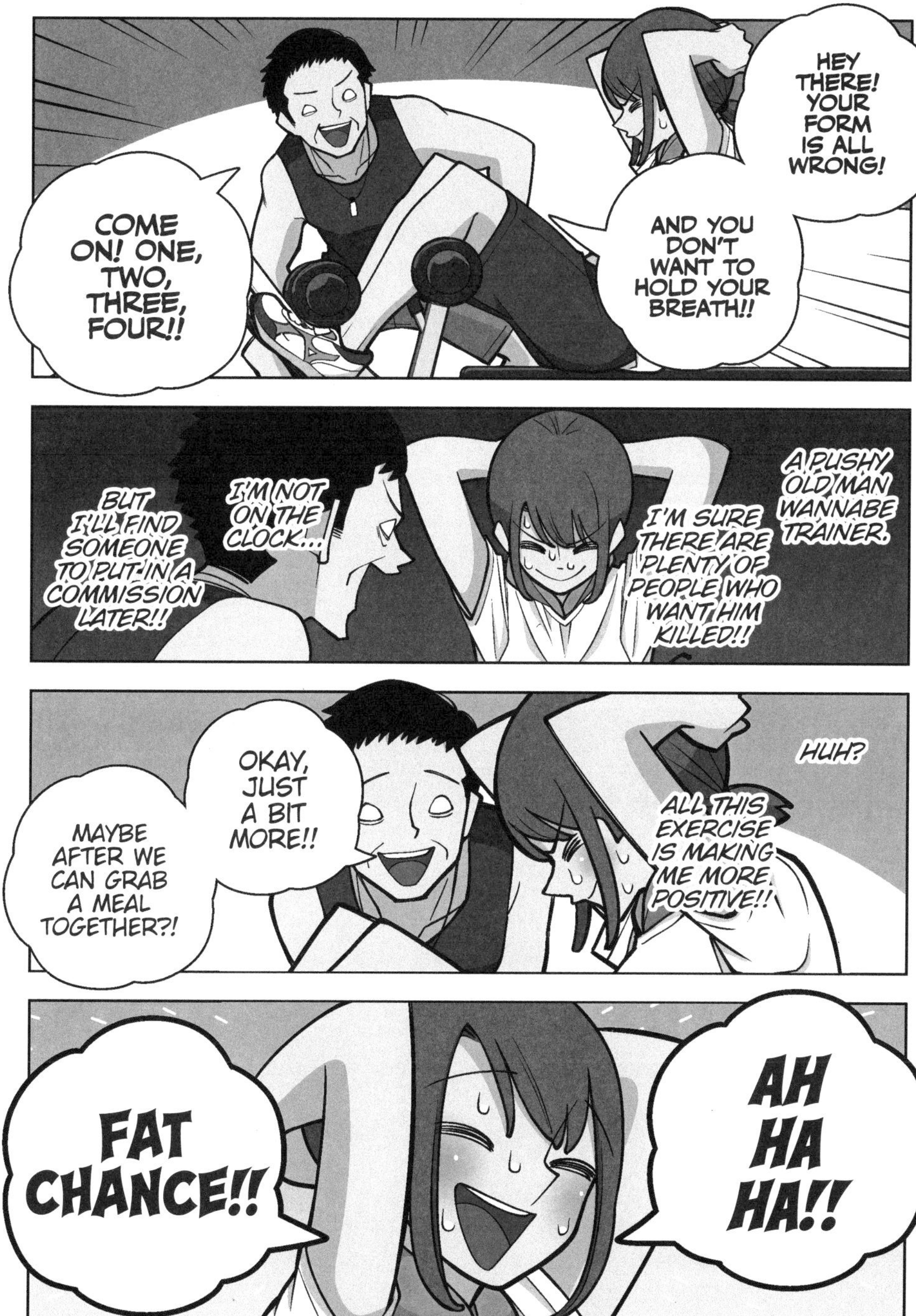
HEY THERE! YOUR FORM IS ALL WRONG!
AND YOU DON'T WANT TO HOLD YOUR BREATH!!
COME ON! ONE, TWO, THREE, FOUR!!
A PUSHY OLD MAN WANNABE TRAINER.
I'M SURE THERE ARE PLENTY OF PEOPLE WHO WANT HIM KILLED!!
I'M NOT ON THE CLOCK...
BUT I'LL FIND SOMEONE TO PUT IN A COMMISSION LATER!!
HUH?
ALL THIS EXERCISE IS MAKING ME MORE POSITIVE!!
OKAY, JUST A BIT MORE!!
MAYBE AFTER WE CAN GRAB A MEAL TOGETHER?!
AH HA HA!!
FAT CHANCE!!

How about NO! ☆

WHAT?

YOU ALREADY QUIT THE GYM?

HUH?

YOU GOTTA SHOW MORE GRIT.

THERE'S THIS ANNOYING GUY THERE...

SORT OF...

I MEAN, I ENJOYED EXERCISING.

I JUST THOUGHT I'D FIND SOMEPLACE ELSE.

FINE. I'LL TRAIN YOU.

STARTING TONIGHT.

DON'T BE LATE, OR YOU'RE DEAD.

☆ —————————————— No chance to veto.

027

SAKURAI-SENPAI SAYS HE'S GOING TO TRAIN ME.

THIS IS A YAKUZA STOREHOUSE.

SO YOU MIGHT FIND A CORPSE IN HERE NOW AND THEN.

I'M GONNA CROAK.

WHICH WILL GET YOU KILLED.

AND THAT MEANS YOU'RE QUICK TO GET TIRED...

YOU JUST LACK PHYSICAL STRENGTH.

YOU'VE GOT POTENTIAL...

WHERE DO WE START?

UM, OKAY, SO...

SURE, IT'S BEEN ROUGH NOW AND THEN, BUT I'VE NEVER FELT LIKE I WAS GOING TO *DIE.*

PUT THIS ON.

I've got a bad feeling about this. ⭐

☆ Women having to wear makeup is one of those secret unwritten rules.

SAKURAI-SAN ISN'T LOOKING DOWN ON ME JUST BECAUSE I'M A WOMAN.

HE SEES ME AS A PERSON!

IT'S EMBARRASSING!!

WANTING HIM TO GO EASY ON ME BECAUSE I'M A WOMAN IS JUST ME BEING SPOILED.

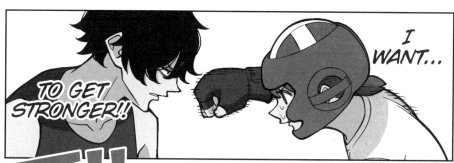

TO GET STRONGER!!

I WANT...

THWACK

Maybe he doesn't even see me as a person, either. ───── ☆

☆ ──────────────────────── **Just needs more training.**

028

Sakuradai - Ikebukuro

Destination · Time · Car · 0

Ikebukuro 8:17 8 Cars 4 1

Due to an incident trains between

Ikebukuro 8:25 8 Cars 4 D

ANOTHER JUMPER.

THE TRAINS'LL BE LATE AGAIN.

IF I DID THAT, AT LEAST I WOULDN'T HAVE TO FACE ANOTHER DAY IN THE OFFICE.

ONCE OR TWICE, I THOUGHT ABOUT JUMPING MYSELF.

BACK WHEN I WAS IN MY LAST JOB...

I SURVIVED.

I RAN AWAY FROM THAT BOSS.

BUT I RAN AWAY FROM THAT COMPANY.

HAVE I REALLY GOTTEN ANY STRONGER...?

I WONDER.

COMPARED TO BACK THEN...

Definitely stronger at murder. ────────── ☆

OUR TARGET THIS TIME...

THERE WASN'T ANY PROOF LINKING THE SUICIDE TO HARASSMENT...

IS A BOSS THAT DROVE AN EMPLOYEE TO SUICIDE LAST YEAR.

SO HE WASN'T PROSECUTED.

......

GOT IT.

VWMM

IT SEEMS HE SMOKES ALONE.

WHEN HE'S DONE, THAT'LL BE THE SIGNAL.

BA-DUMP

BA-DUMP

BA-DUMP

WHAT THE HECK...? WHY AM I MORE NERVOUS THAN USUAL?

AND COMPARED TO BACK THEN, I'M...

BUT I KILLED HIM.

MAYBE BECAUSE IT REMINDS ME OF *MY* LAST BOSS.

VWMM

☆ —————————— **#PTSD: Panicked Tiger, Scared Donkey.**

Oblivious to the consequences of his actions. ───── ☆

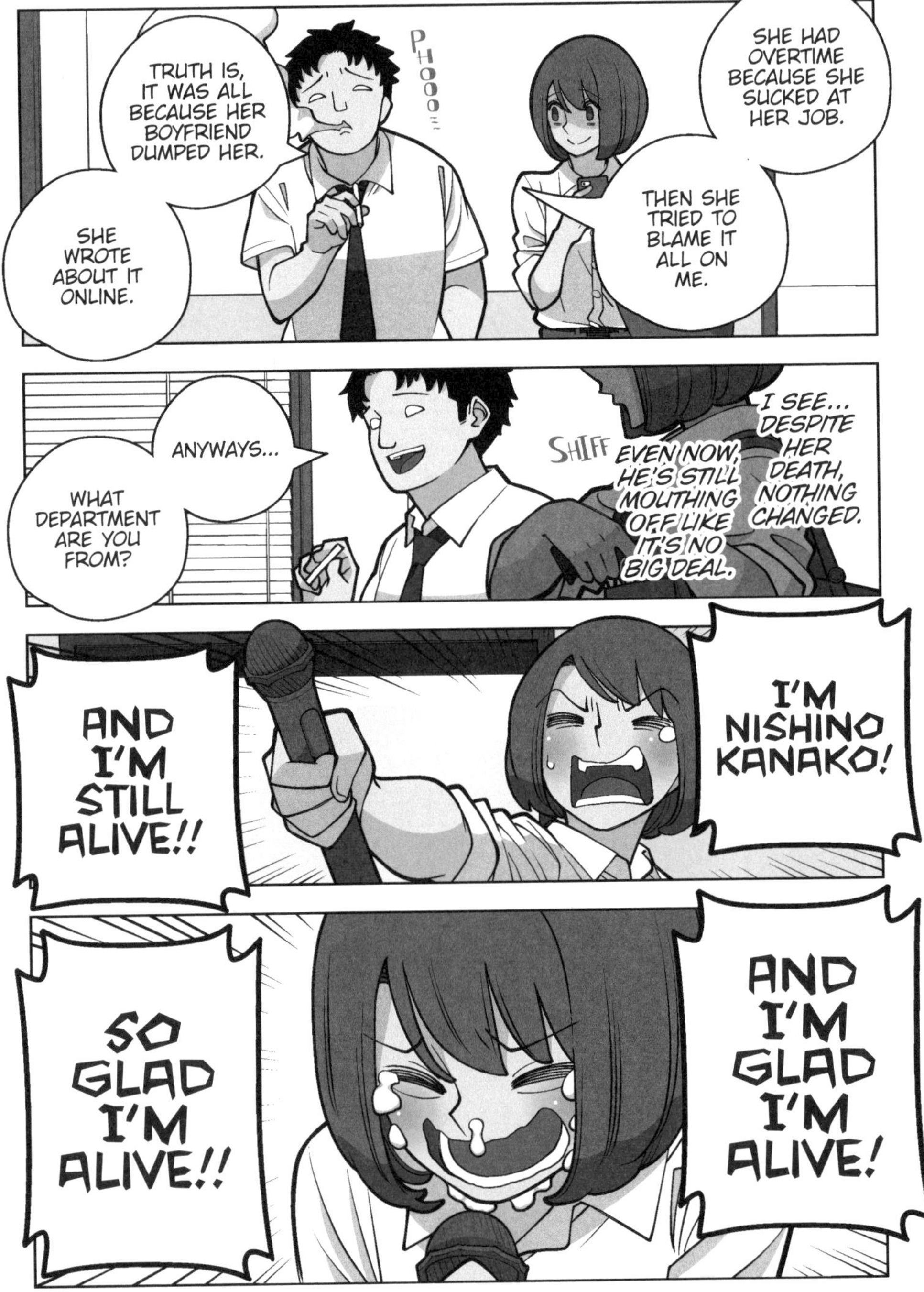

SHE HAD OVERTIME BECAUSE SHE SUCKED AT HER JOB.
THEN SHE TRIED TO BLAME IT ALL ON ME.
PHOOO
TRUTH IS, IT WAS ALL BECAUSE HER BOYFRIEND DUMPED HER.
SHE WROTE ABOUT IT ONLINE.
I SEE... DESPITE HER DEATH, NOTHING CHANGED.
EVEN NOW, HE'S STILL MOUTHING OFF LIKE IT'S NO BIG DEAL.
SHIFF
ANYWAYS...
WHAT DEPARTMENT ARE YOU FROM?
I'M NISHINO KANAKO!
AND I'M STILL ALIVE!!
AND I'M GLAD I'M ALIVE!
SO GLAD I'M ALIVE!!

☆ —— We're glad, too.

Happy Kanako's
Killer Life

Prawn-
haps I
screwed
up?

Happy Kanako's
Killer Life

Feline
fur-
ious!!

Bonus

Shiver with An...tici...pation! ──────── ☆

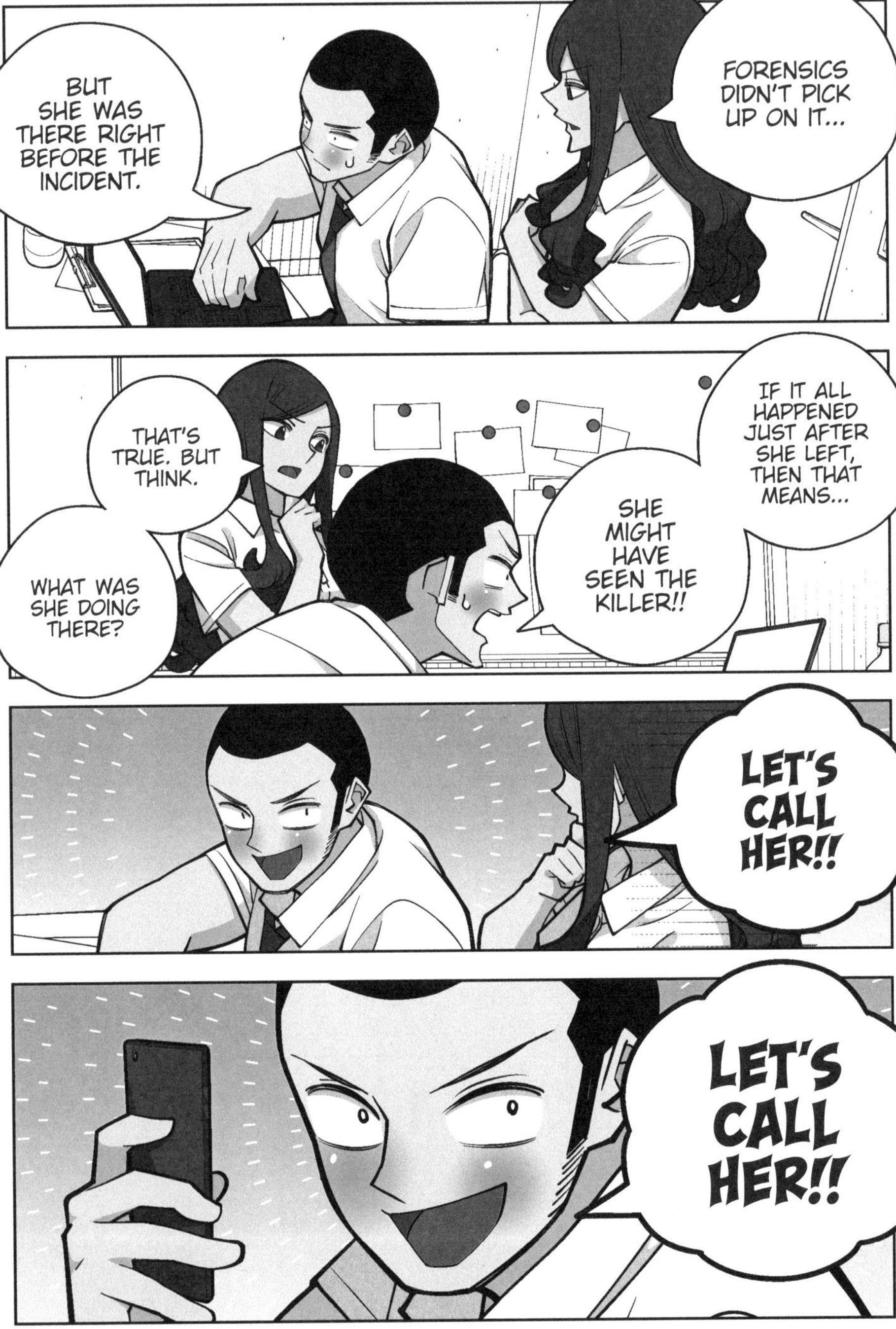
FORENSICS DIDN'T PICK UP ON IT...
BUT SHE WAS THERE RIGHT BEFORE THE INCIDENT.
IF IT ALL HAPPENED JUST AFTER SHE LEFT, THEN THAT MEANS...
SHE MIGHT HAVE SEEN THE KILLER!!
THAT'S TRUE. BUT THINK.
WHAT WAS SHE DOING THERE?
LET'S CALL HER!!
LET'S CALL HER!!

PHEW...

I SANG SO MUCH...

EVER SINCE BECOMING A HITMAN, MY LIFE'S CHANGED A LOT.

AND I'VE CHANGED A LOT MYSELF.

I WISH I COULD GO SEE MY PAST SELF, AND TELL HER HOW MUCH BETTER THE FUTURE IS GOING TO--

VRRRRRR

POLICE
Mobile

When they come for you! ⎯⎯⎯⎯⎯⎯⎯⎯⎯⎯⎯⎯⎯⎯ ☆

THIS IS TAKEHARA WITH THE POLICE!!

AH!!

SORRY TO CALL SO LATE AT NIGHT!!

I'M ACTUALLY CALLING ON BEHALF OF DETECTIVE OMORI.

SHE NOTICED YOU WERE AT THE SCENE OF ANOTHER INCIDENT RECENTLY...

SO THAT'S WHY I'M CALLING!!

WH... WHAT??

WHERE WAS THAT??

THAT I HONESTLY HAVE NO IDEA...!!

WHERE, INDEED!

THERE HAVE BEEN SO MANY "INCIDENTS" LATELY...

☆ ——————————————— She's a walking crime scene.

Just a bit longer, please! ⭐

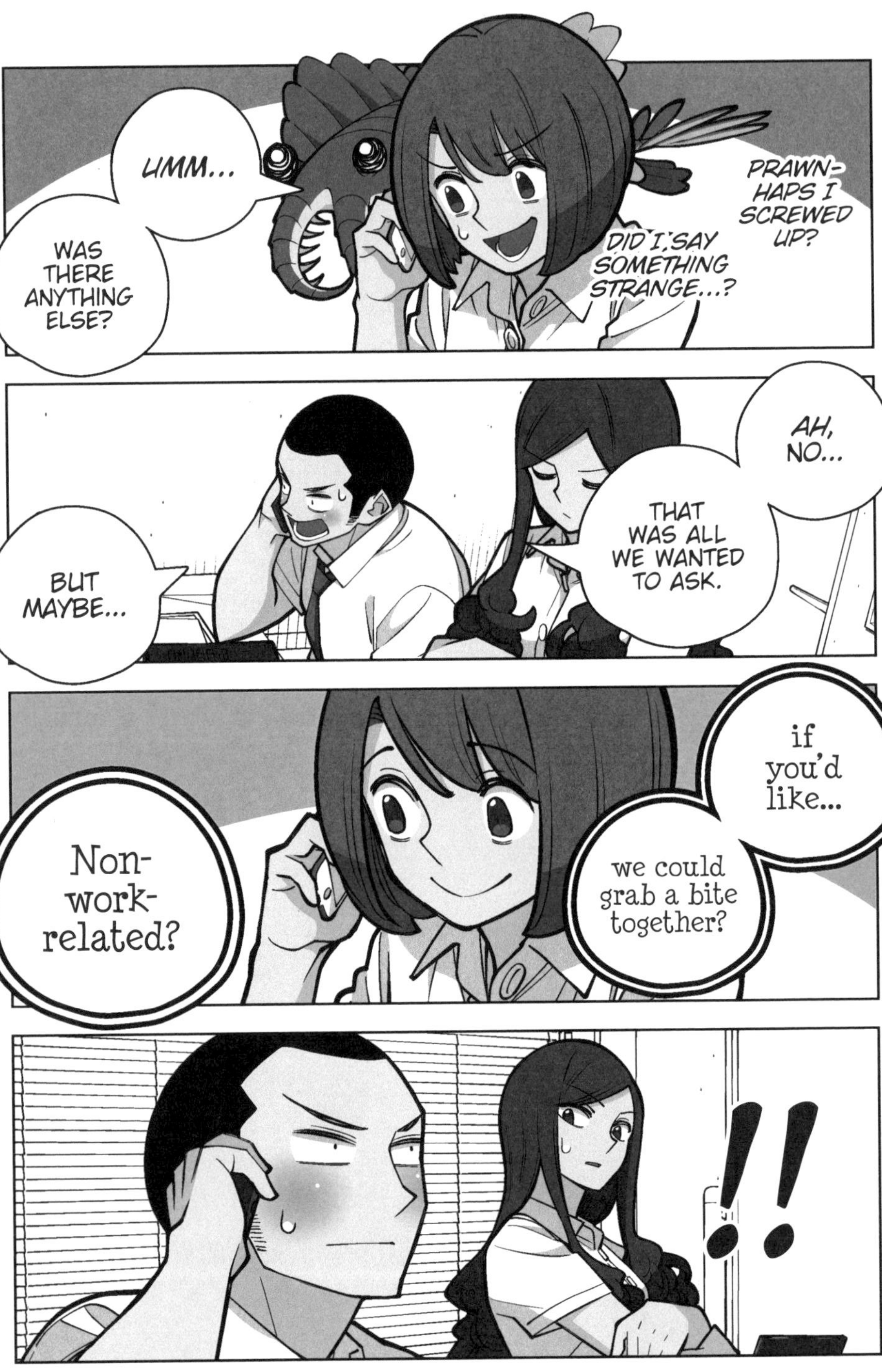
UMM...
WAS THERE ANYTHING ELSE?
DID I SAY SOMETHING STRANGE...?
PRAWN-HAPS I SCREWED UP?
AH, NO...
THAT WAS ALL WE WANTED TO ASK.
BUT MAYBE...
if you'd like...
we could grab a bite together?
Non-work-related?
!!

☆ What did he just say?!

NOTHING TO DO WITH THE CASE OR WORK.

JUST ME AND YOU.

HAVING A MEAL TOGETHER.

THIS IS UN-BUNNY-BELIEVABLE...

THIS IS DEFINITELY WORK-RELATED...!!

WHAT ELSE WOULD A DETECTIVE WANT WITH SOMEONE LIKE ME?

only if you're okay with it.

Really, uh...

Then...

Okay.

What did she just say?! ─────────────────── ☆

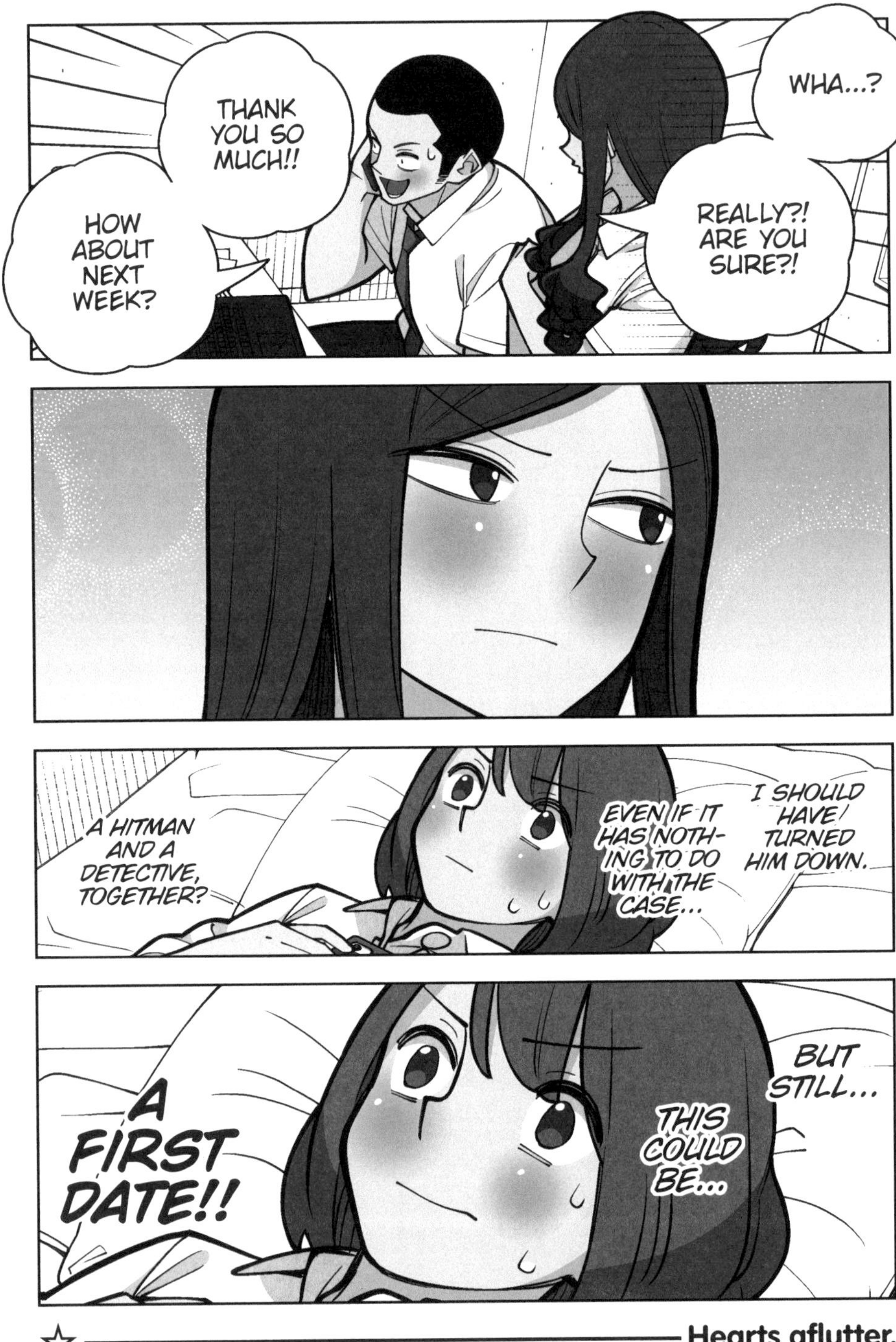
WHA...?
REALLY?! ARE YOU SURE?!
THANK YOU SO MUCH!!
HOW ABOUT NEXT WEEK?
I SHOULD HAVE TURNED HIM DOWN.
EVEN IF IT HAS NOTHING TO DO WITH THE CASE...
A HITMAN AND A DETECTIVE, TOGETHER?
BUT STILL...
THIS COULD BE...
A FIRST DATE!!

☆ Hearts aflutter.

Happy Kanako's
Killer Life

Happy Kanako's
Killer Life

029

Chest-Pounding Excitement! ——————————— ☆

YOU SEEM IN AWFULLY HIGH SPIRITS.

NISHINO.

......

YOU'VE BEEN SMILING ALL DAY.

WELL...

FLINCH

WH-WHY DO YOU THINK THAT??

WHA?!

YOU'VE FOUND YOURSELF A BOY-FRIEND?

COULD IT BE...

LIKE *THAT* WOULD EVER HAPPEN!!

WHOA! COME ON, BOSS!!

☆ Still cruising De-Nile river. ─────────────!!

I'VE GOT TO STAY PROFESSIONAL IN THE WORKPLACE!!

CAN'T LET MYSELF GET TOO EXCITED!!

I'VE GOT TO KEEP IT TOGETHER.

THIS MIGHT STILL JUST BE PART OF THE INVESTIGATION.

I STILL DON'T KNOW IF THIS IS REALLY A DATE.

AND SHE ACTUALLY DID IT!!

I TOLD HER TO SEND ME NUDES...

LOOK AT THIS!!

I PROBABLY SHOULDN'T KILL THIS GUY, HUH?

IF I'M UNDER ACTIVE INVESTIGATION...

It's hard being unpopular. ———————————☆

I JUST SEND 'EM THAT DUDE'S NUDES THAT I FOUND ONLINE.

I'VE GOT THIS TWENTY-SOMETHING HAIRDRESSER PROFILE.

I TOLD HER I'D TRADE PICS.

I CAN'T BELIEVE SHE FELL FOR IT.

EVEN NICE ADULTS LIKE ME HAVE TO BE CAREFUL.

TAP TAP

Contact the target.

THIS WORLD IS FULL OF NASTY PEOPLE.

THAT'S RIGHT...

LET'S GO PICK UP OUR TUITION FEES!!

OH!! IT'S FROM THE GIRL!!

SHE SAYS SHE'S BRINGING THE MONEY!!

SPLOOSH

THIS WORLD REALLY CAN BE A SCARY PLACE!

 ─────────── **Another snake in the river.**

030

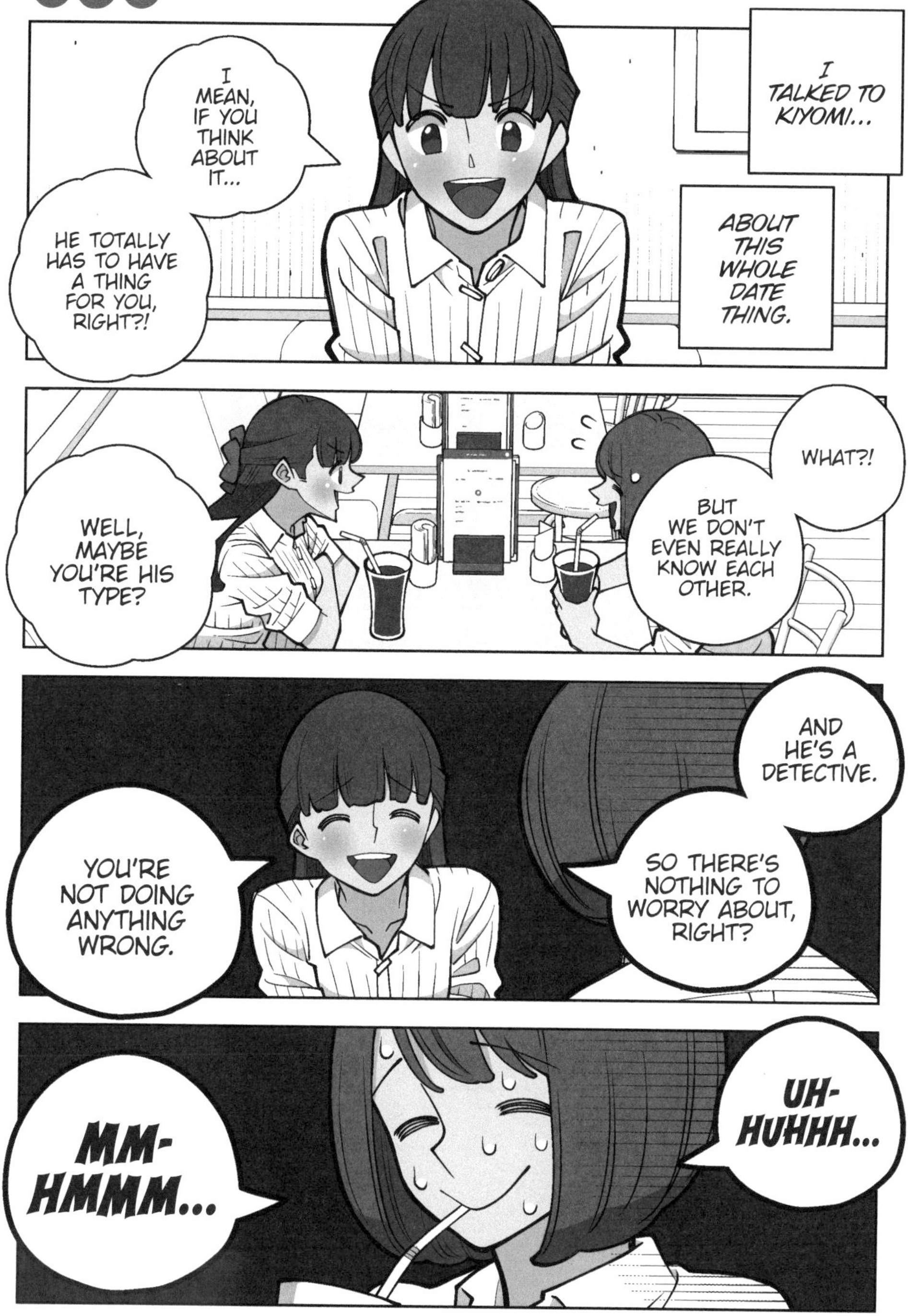

I TALKED TO KIYOMI...
ABOUT THIS WHOLE DATE THING.
I MEAN, IF YOU THINK ABOUT IT...
HE TOTALLY HAS TO HAVE A THING FOR YOU, RIGHT?!
WHAT?!
BUT WE DON'T EVEN REALLY KNOW EACH OTHER.
WELL, MAYBE YOU'RE HIS TYPE?
AND HE'S A DETECTIVE.
SO THERE'S NOTHING TO WORRY ABOUT, RIGHT?
YOU'RE NOT DOING ANYTHING WRONG.
UH-HUHHH...
MM-HMMM...

Mum's the word! ☆

☆ ——————— Sounds like those might lead to new business.

Nothing corporal punishment can't solve! ———————— ☆

Knock 'em dead with the vocals!

031

HEY.

YOU SHOULDN'T BE WORN OUT THIS QUICKLY.

LATELY, IT FEELS LIKE SAKURAI-SAN'S TRAINING...

HAS BEEN GETTING TOUGHER.

WHEN YOU FIRST JOINED, YOU LOOKED LIKE DEATH WARMED OVER.

BUT THIS PAST WEEK YOU'VE BEEN ALMOST GIDDY.

I'M SORRY...

BECAUSE OF MY ATTITUDE!!

HE'S BEEN GOING HARDER ON ME!!

CRAP, I'M GONNA GET RAILED...

AND I DON'T WANT ANY BRUISES!!

BUT...

TOMORROW NIGHT'S MY DATE!

Incredibly giddy! ———————————————————— ☆

☆ When you ask if I don't understand, I'm too afraid to answer!

ARE YOU REALLY JUST A NATURAL?

ENOUGH WITH THE FLATTERY.

HOW DO YOU REMEMBER IT ALL?

SO I'D DO WHATEVER I COULD TO AVOID MAKING HIM ANGRY.

I WAS JUST ALWAYS AFRAID OF MY LAST BOSS GETTING MAD AT ME.

NO... DEFINITELY NOT A NATURAL.

AND IF I DON'T RECALL SOMETHING, I CAN GO BACK OVER IT.

I WRITE DOWN WHATEVER PEOPLE SAY AND DO.

I HAVE A HABIT.

DOING MY BEST TO MAKE SURE PEOPLE DON'T GET MAD AT ME!

OTHER THAN THAT, IT'S JUST...

She just doesn't want to be yelled at. ──────── ☆

NO, WELL...

I'VE NEVER REALLY BEEN RECOGNIZED FOR WHAT I DO BEFORE...

AND *THAT'S* WHY YOU CAN DO THE JOB?

.....

THE PEOPLE AROUND YOU CLEARLY HAD NO EYE FOR TALENT.

IN THAT CASE...

PRAISE ME FOR THE FIRST TIME...?

DID... DID SAKURAI-SAN JUST...

I'LL KILL YOU.

WHAT ARE YOU LOOKING AT?

☆ ———————————————————— **Understood.**

RUMORS ARE FLOATING THROUGH THE UNDERWORLD...

ABOUT THE KILLER KNOWN AS "K."

HEY THERE, MISS.

HOW'S K DOING?

HA HA.

AS DISCREET AS EVER, I SEE.

THERE'S NO "K" IN OUR COMPANY!!

I'VE TOLD YOU, SIR.

IS THIS K PERSON CRAZY?

ALL DONE INCREDIBLY BLATANTLY, BUT LEAVING NO EVIDENCE.

SHOOTINGS AND POISONINGS DONE OUT IN PUBLIC.

THERE'S BEEN STORIES LATELY.

ISN'T THAT AMAZING?!!

OH WOW!

I agree, must be crazy. ─────────────── ☆

THEY'LL HAVE TO BE CAREFUL, THOUGH.

EVEN UNDERWORLD TYPES ARE LOOKING FOR K NOW.

IT'S NOT JUST THE COPS.

BEFORE I BECOME A TARGET...

THERE ARE PEOPLE WHO WOULDN'T MIND SEEING ME DEAD.

I'D BETTER GET K ON MY SIDE.

YEAH, WELL.

IT'S A SMALL WORLD, AFTER ALL...

EH... BUT...

YOU DON'T KNOW WHO THEY ARE...

ANYWAY...

YOU SHOULD BE CAREFUL, TOO.

☆ ——————————————— **It's hard being famous.**

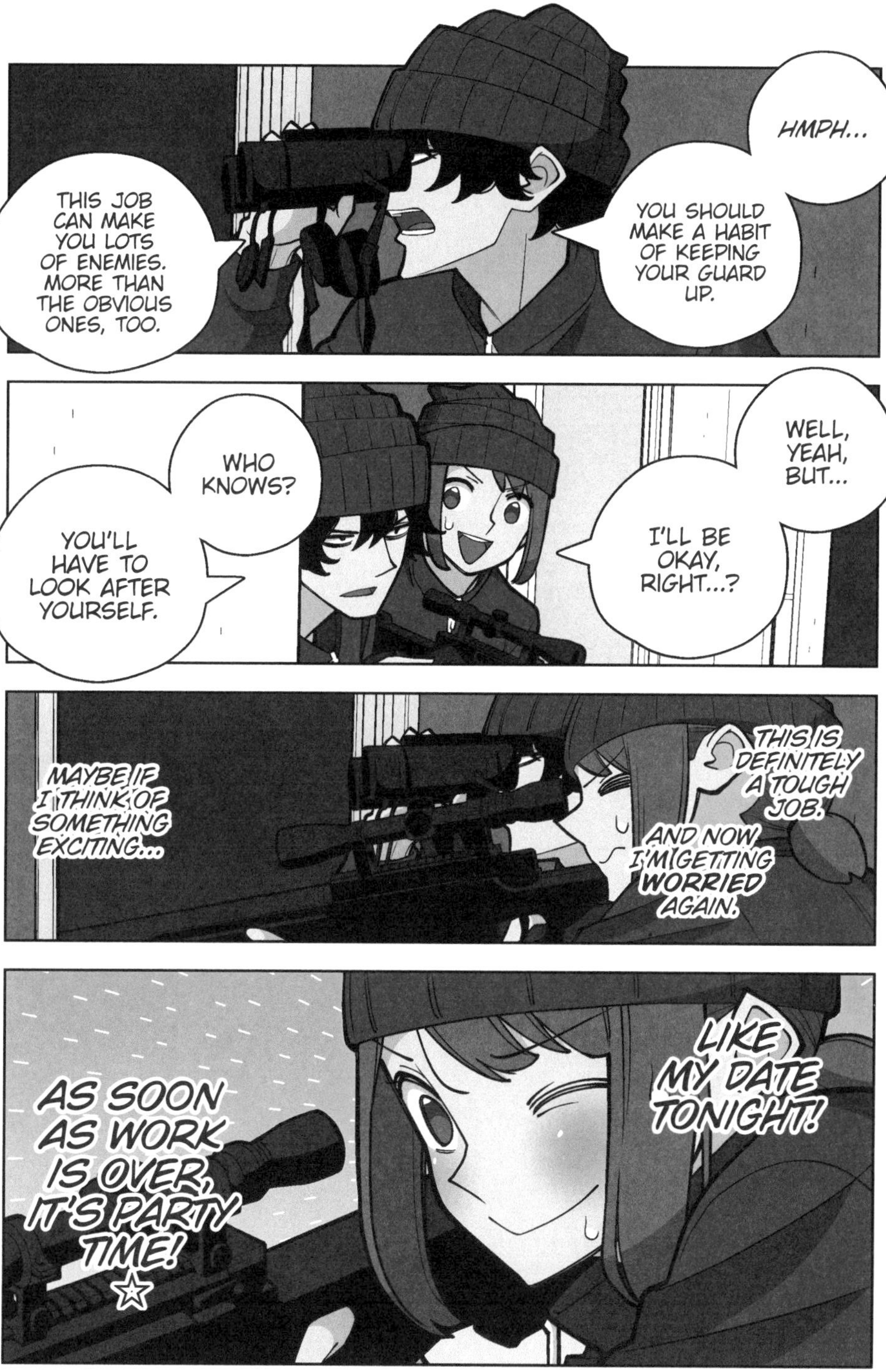
THIS JOB CAN MAKE YOU LOTS OF ENEMIES. MORE THAN THE OBVIOUS ONES, TOO.
HMPH...
YOU SHOULD MAKE A HABIT OF KEEPING YOUR GUARD UP.
WHO KNOWS?
YOU'LL HAVE TO LOOK AFTER YOURSELF.
WELL, YEAH, BUT...
I'LL BE OKAY, RIGHT...?
MAYBE IF I THINK OF SOMETHING EXCITING...
THIS IS DEFINITELY A TOUGH JOB.
AND NOW I'M GETTING WORRIED AGAIN.
AS SOON AS WORK IS OVER, IT'S PARTY TIME! ☆
LIKE MY DATE TONIGHT!

Friday is Battle Night. ☆

THEY'RE HERE.

IF THE DEAL GOES SOUTH, HE'LL GIVE US A SIGNAL.

THEN TAKE THE SHOT.

THIS IS TURTLELY NUTS...

WHAT DO YOU TALK ABOUT ON A DATE...?

CAN I TALK ABOUT SUPERHERO SHOWS...?

HOLD UP, THIS DATE IS JUST A MEAL, RIGHT...?

AFTER THE MEAL WE'RE NOT DOING ANYTHING ELSE, RIGHT...?

UH...

ARE WE?

 Unceasing delusions.

NO SIGNAL YET.

I'M GOING TO TAKE A LOOK AROUND.

THERE MIGHT BE OTHERS IN HIDING.

THAT DETECTIVE...

PHYSICALLY, HE'S NOT REALLY MY TYPE.

MAYBE IT'LL WORK OUT.

BUT HE SEEMS NICE, AND WE LIKE SIMILAR THINGS.

!

AND THEN IF ALL GOES WELL, MAYBE I COULD QUIT THIS JOB AND--

Sakurai- *saaaaaaan!*

A SNIPER.

THEY KNEW WE'D BE HERE.

HUH?!

WHAT WAS THAT?!

DIDN'T HIT ANYTHING VITAL.

MORE IMPORTANTLY, THE SNIPER'S LOCATION IS...

W-WAIT... SAKURAI-SAN...!!

WERE YOU SHOT?!

BUT I STILL LET MYSELF GET CARRIED AWAY...

HE TOLD ME TO LOOK AFTER MYSELF.

THIS IS MY FAULT...

I'M WORTHLESS...

LESS THAN A COCKROACH...

☆ ——————— **Sense of self-worth: 100% Shattered.**

As sneaky as a cockroach. ────────────────── ☆

NO ONE'S ANSWERING...

......

TAK

!

BECAUSE THEY'RE ALL DEAD.

ARE YOU...

NO WAY...

......

"K"...?

Awakening!

Happy Kanako's
Killer Life

Hamming it up!!

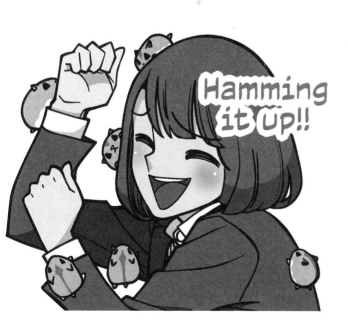

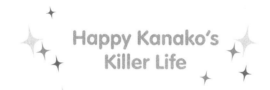

Happy Kanako's
Killer Life

The bulldog blues.

Bonus

Hearing that now brings nothing but sadness. —————— ☆

HEY...

DON'T YOU HAVE SOMEWHERE TO BE?

BUT...

IT WAS PART OF MY DUTIES AS YOUR SUPPORT.

JUST ANOTHER PART OF THE JOB.

IT'S MY FAULT YOU GOT...!!

WATCH CLOSELY AND REMEMBER.

NISHINO, THIS IS YOUR FIRST TIME SEEING A WOUND GET TREATED, RIGHT?

TIME TO CLOSE YOU UP, SAKURAI.

THANK YOU, SIR!!

I'VE GOT THE KOALAFICA-TIONS!!

☆ ────────── **Boss always finds room for people.**

He grows on you as you get to know him. ─────── ☆

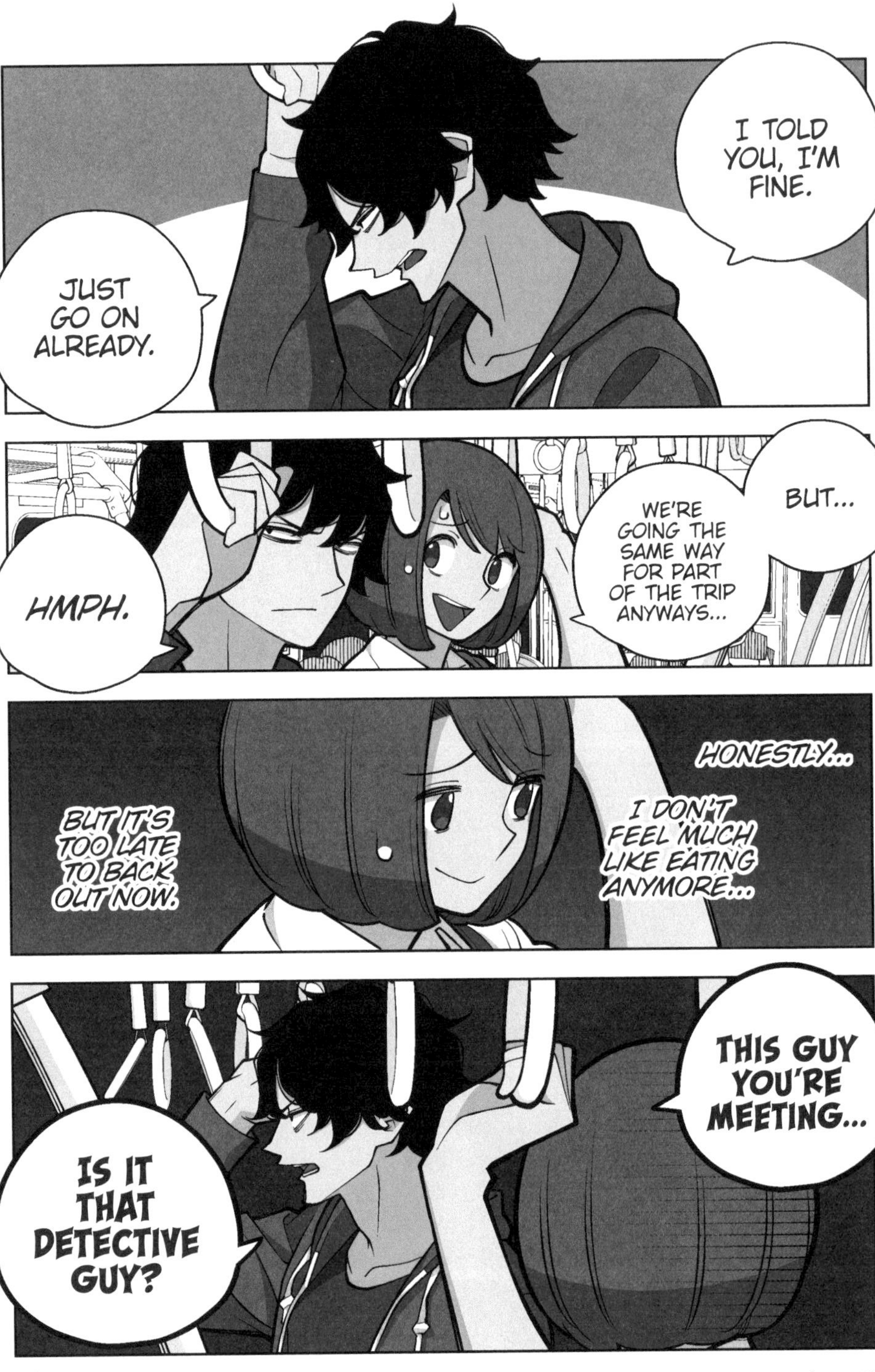
I TOLD YOU, I'M FINE.
JUST GO ON ALREADY.
BUT...
WE'RE GOING THE SAME WAY FOR PART OF THE TRIP ANYWAYS...
HMPH.
HONESTLY...
I DON'T FEEL MUCH LIKE EATING ANYMORE...
BUT IT'S TOO LATE TO BACK OUT NOW.
THIS GUY YOU'RE MEETING...
IS IT THAT DETECTIVE GUY?

☆ — Found out!

He grew on me as I got to know him. ────────── ☆

YOU DON'T KNOW THAT MANY PEOPLE.

THERE WAS NO ONE ELSE IT COULD BE.

HOW DO YOU KNOW THAT...?!

I'M NOT SAYING NOT TO GO.

BUT DO YOU THINK YOU CAN KEEP A SECRET?

BUT... I...

IF YOU DON'T THINK I SHOULD GO, I WON'T...

BUT I DIDN'T REALLY...

I KNOW THAT IF I'M FOUND OUT I'LL GET GOT...

WELL, THAT'S...

YOU NEED TO DROP THIS DETECTIVE.

IF YOU ASK ME...

☆ —————————————— **Say what now?**

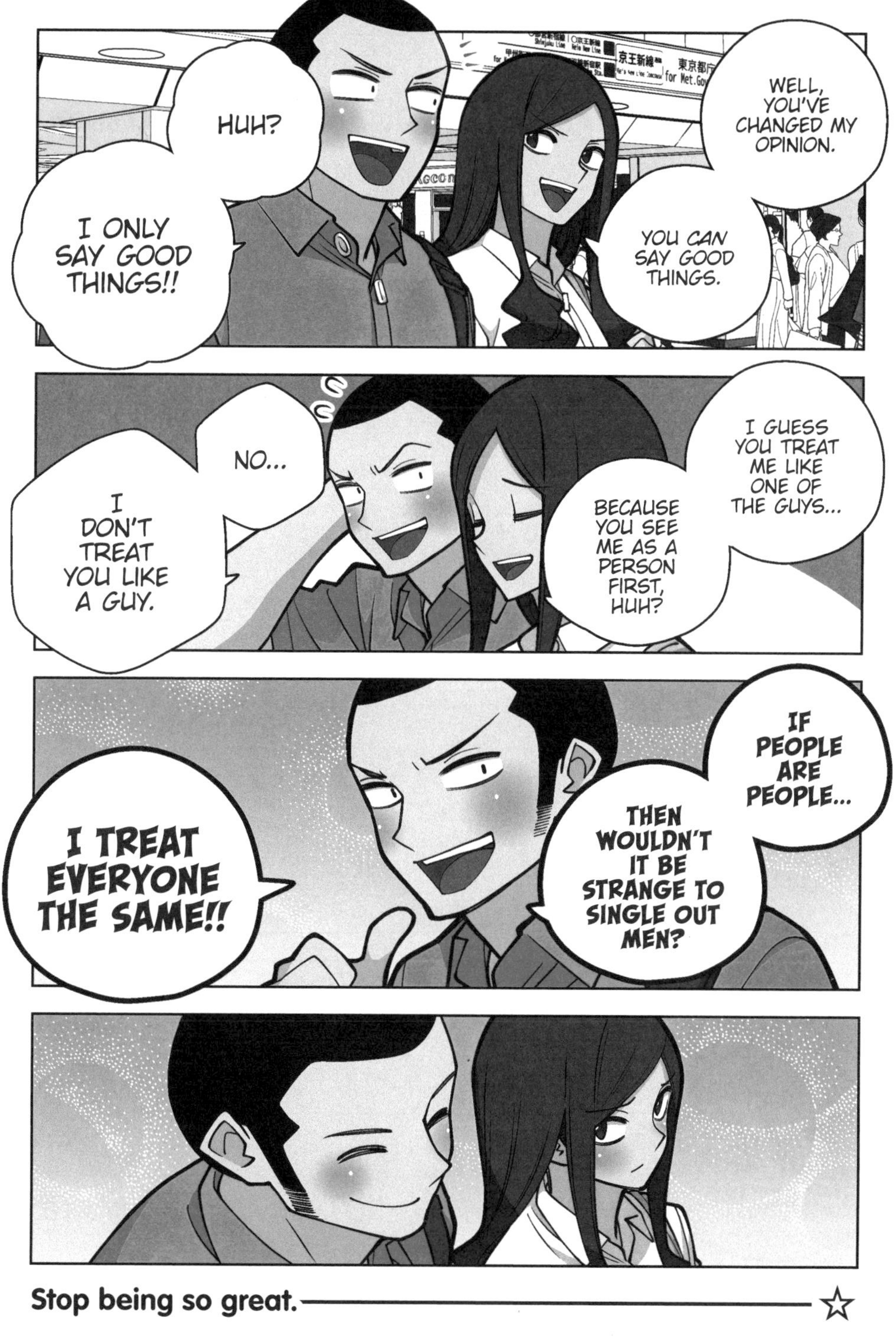
WELL, YOU'VE CHANGED MY OPINION.
YOU CAN SAY GOOD THINGS.
HUH?
I ONLY SAY GOOD THINGS!!
I GUESS YOU TREAT ME LIKE ONE OF THE GUYS...
BECAUSE YOU SEE ME AS A PERSON FIRST, HUH?
NO...
I DON'T TREAT YOU LIKE A GUY.
IF PEOPLE ARE PEOPLE...
THEN WOULDN'T IT BE STRANGE TO SINGLE OUT MEN?
I TREAT EVERYONE THE SAME!!

Stop being so great. ☆

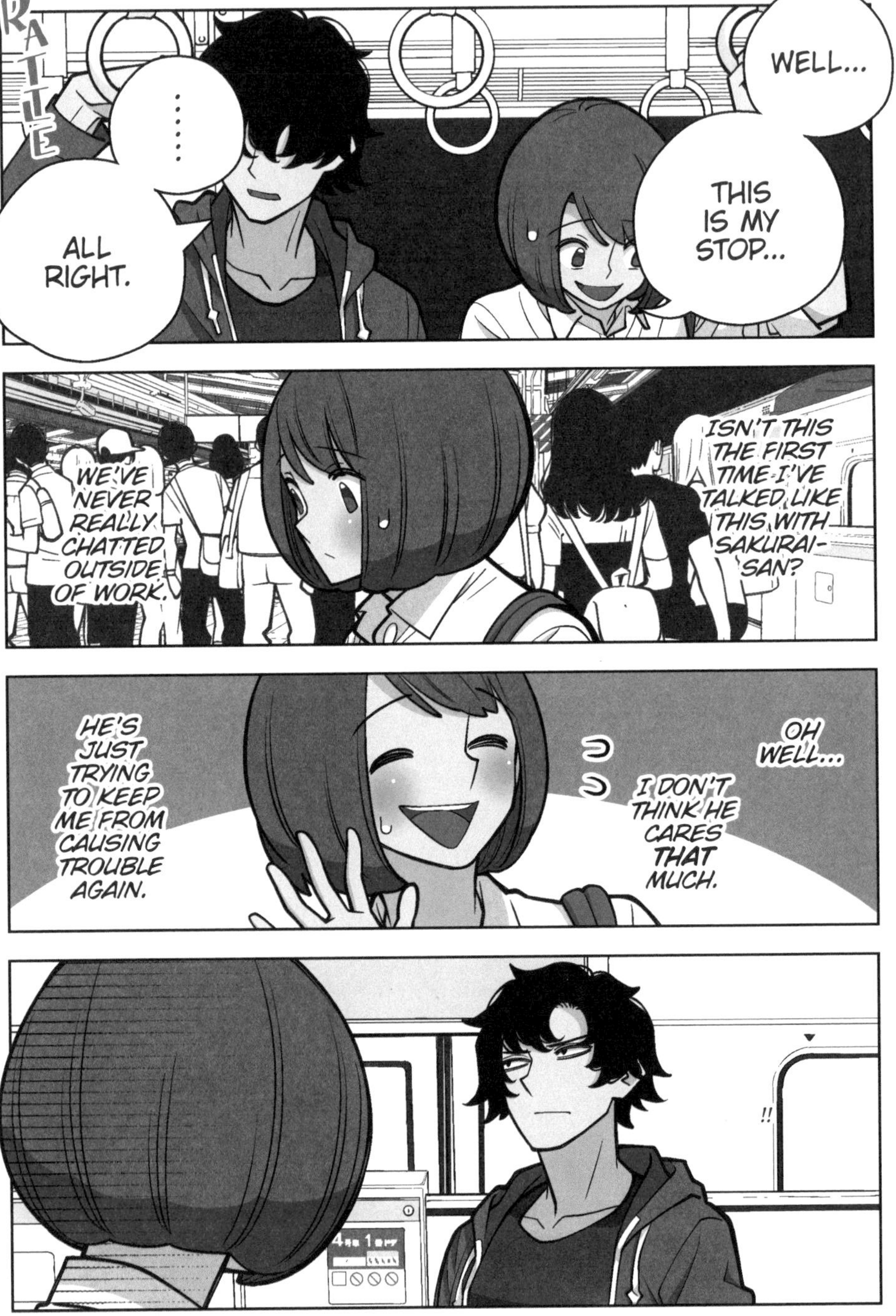
RATTLE
WELL...
THIS IS MY STOP...
......
ALL RIGHT.
ISN'T THIS THE FIRST TIME I'VE TALKED LIKE THIS WITH SAKURAI-SAN?
WE'VE NEVER REALLY CHATTED OUTSIDE OF WORK.
OH WELL...
I DON'T THINK HE CARES THAT MUCH.
HE'S JUST TRYING TO KEEP ME FROM CAUSING TROUBLE AGAIN.
!!

☆ He's here!

WHY DID YOU...?

SAKURAI-SAN...?

YOU'RE RIGHT!!

WHO'S THAT GUY WITH HER?

HEY.

ISN'T THAT HER?

HELLO!!

......

AH!! TAKEHARA-SAN...

......

UMM... DO YOU TWO WORK TOGETHER?!

I'M TAKEHARA, NISHINO-SAN'S FRIEND!!

NICE TO MEET YOU!!

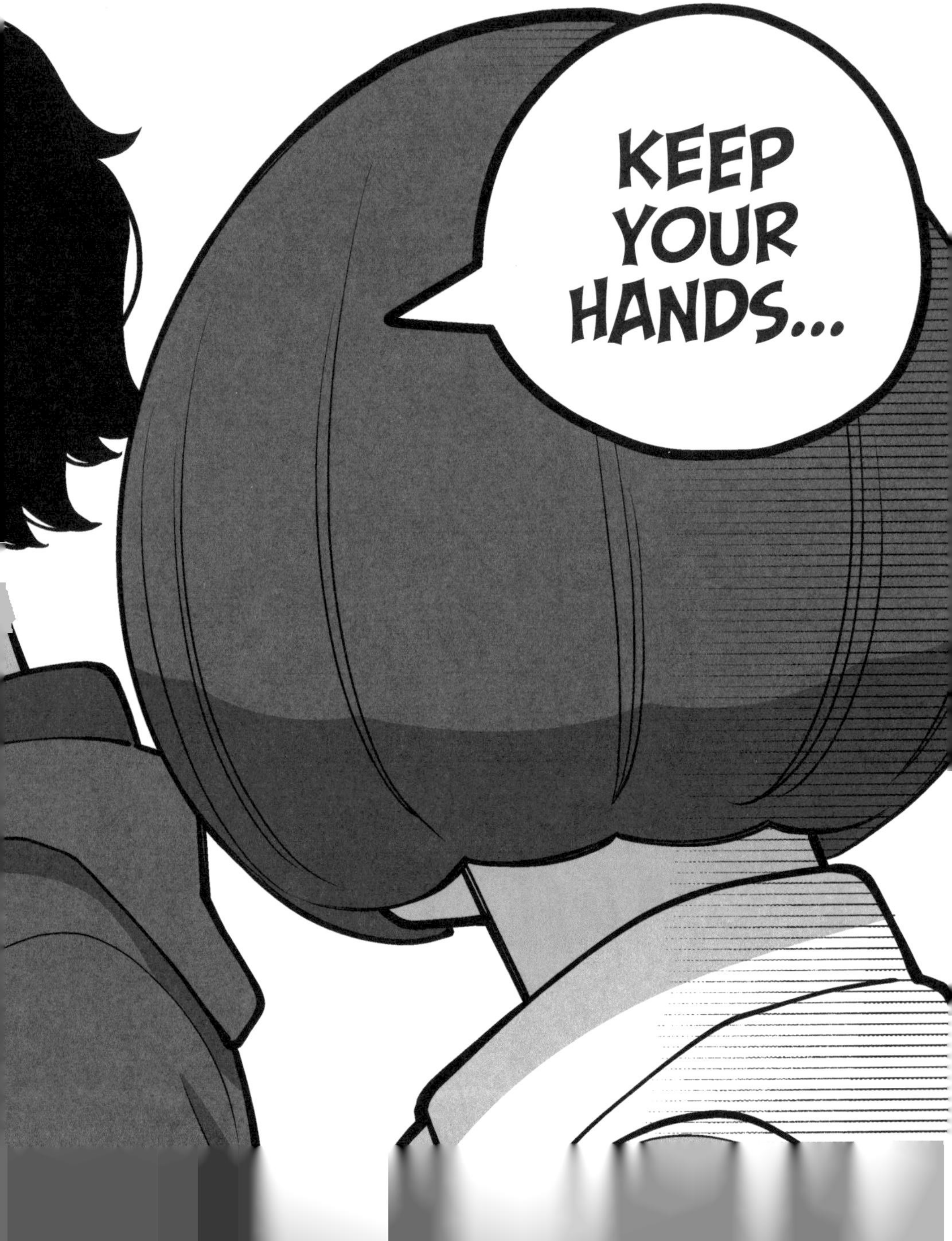
KEEP YOUR HANDS...

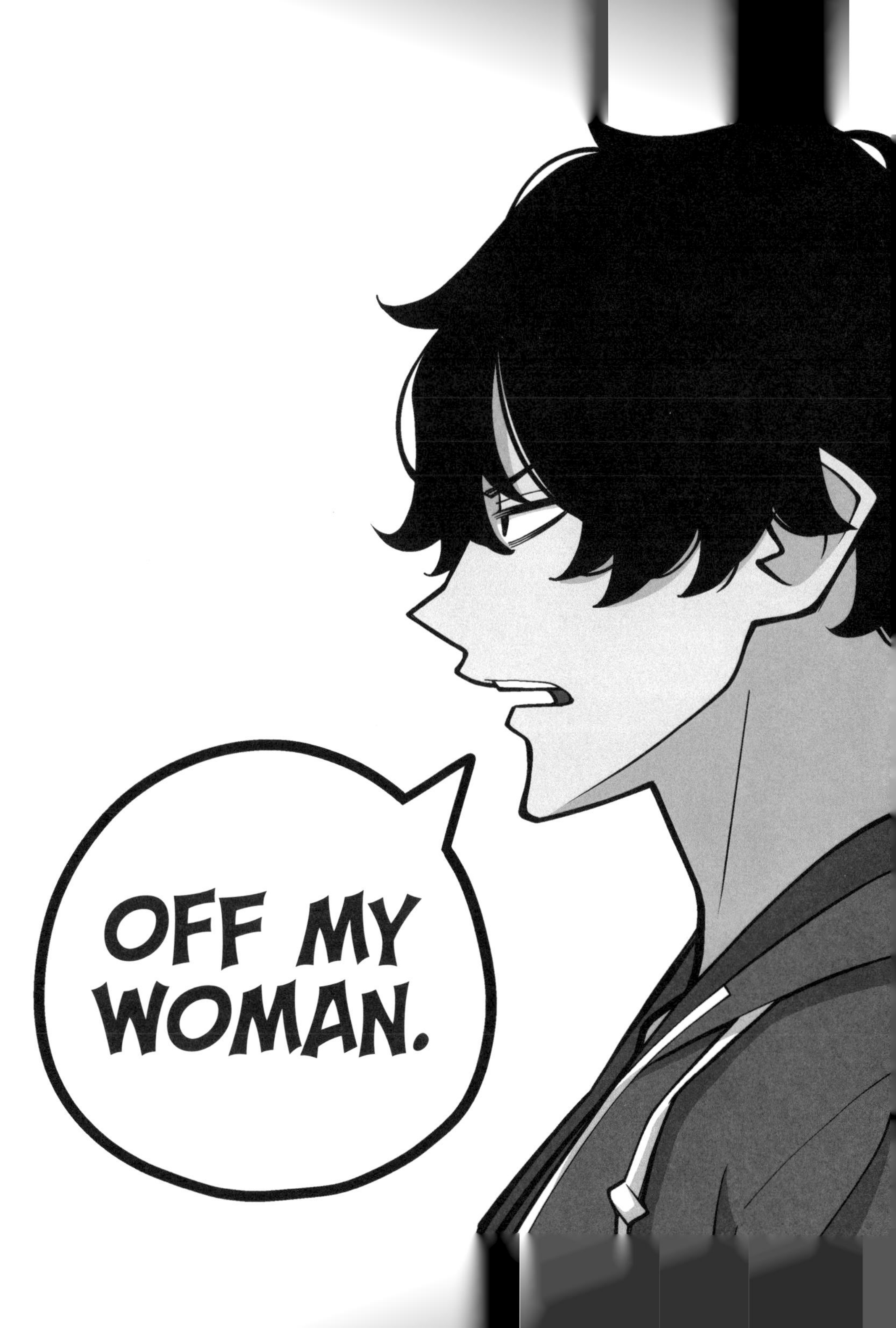
OFF MY WOMAN.

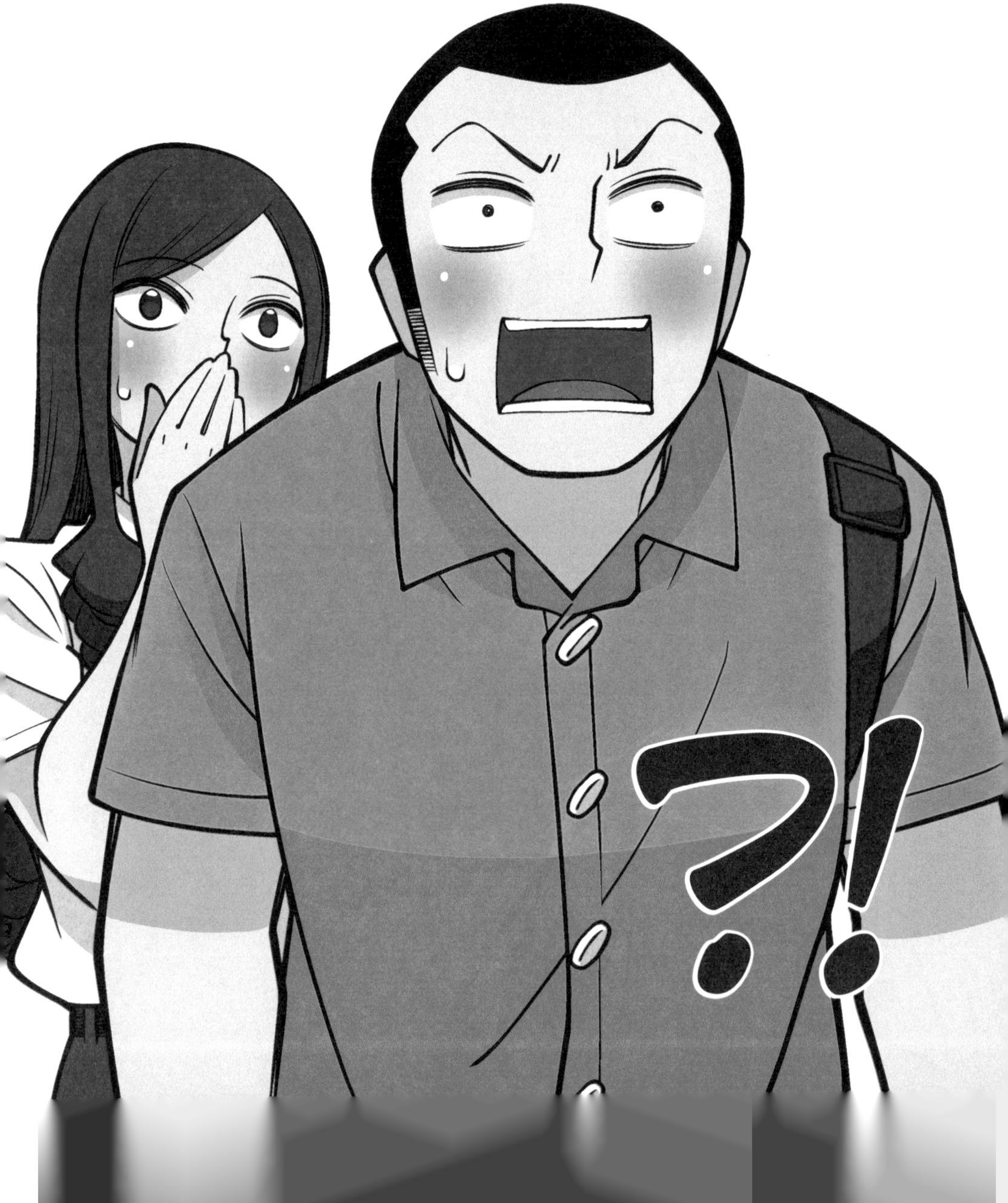
?!

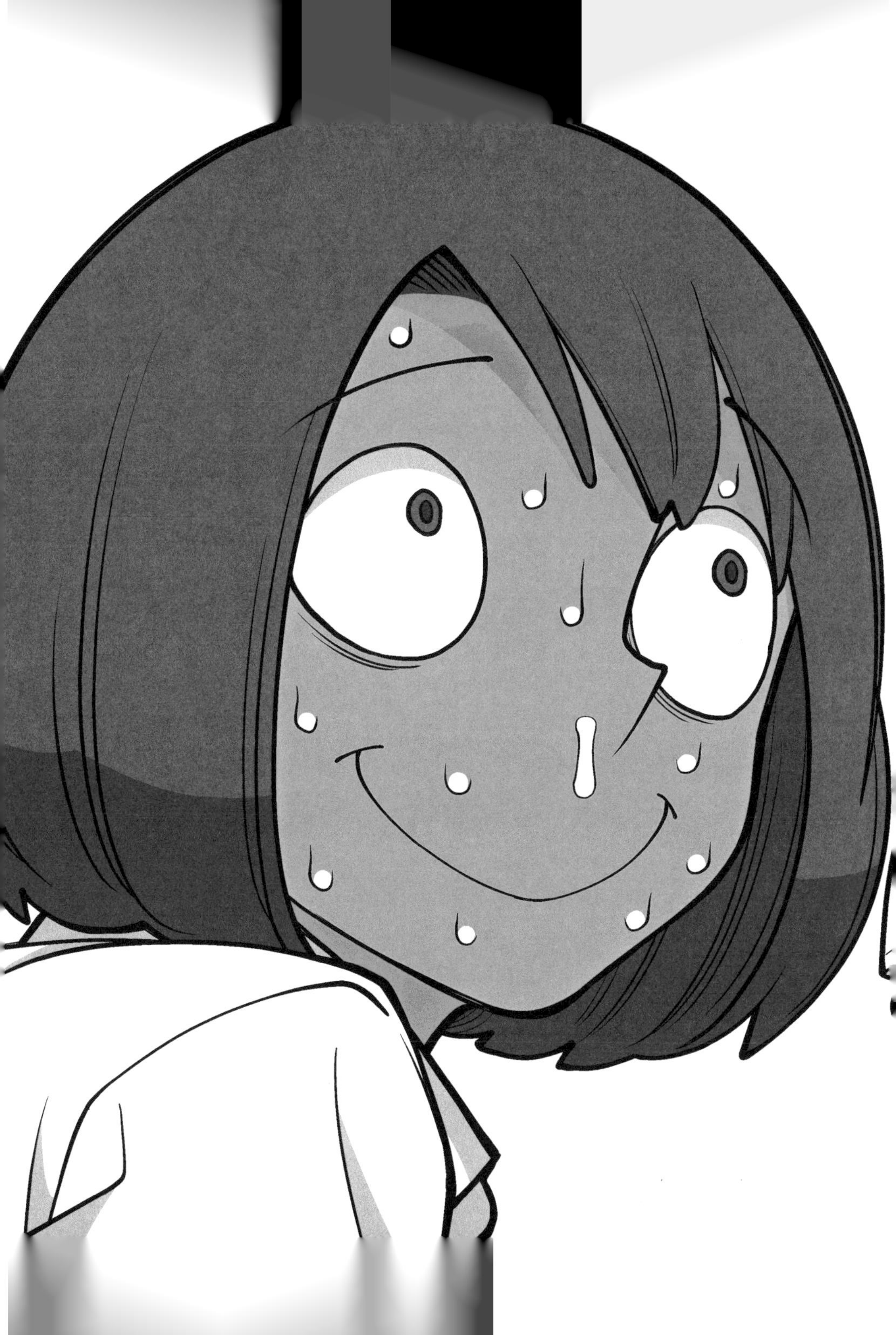

EH?!

BUT...!!

LET'S GO.

AND FIND YOURSELF SOMEONE BETTER.

TAKE THIS OPPORTUNITY TO CUT THINGS OFF.

NISHINO-SAN...

．．．．．．

☆ ──────────────── To be continued!

Happy Kanako's
Killer Life

Thank you so much for reading!! I hope this helped nourish ur fighting spirit!!